CityPack
New York

KATE SEKULES

Adopted New Yorker Kate Sekules writes about travel, food and fitness for many magazines, including The New Yorker, Travel & Leisure, Health & Fitness, Food & Wine *and* Harper's Bazaar. *She is also a co-author of Fodor's* New York City, *author of* By Night: New York, *and a consultant on the US Mobil Travel Guides.*

City-centre map continues on inside back cover

AA Publishing

Contents

About this book...4

About this book

KEY TO SYMBOLS

✚	map reference on the fold-out map accompanying this book (see below)	🚌	nearest bus route
✉	address	🚢	nearest riverboat or ferry stop
☎	telephone number	♿	facilities for visitors with disabilities
🕐	opening times	✋	admission charge
🍴	restaurant or café on premises or nearby	↔	other nearby places of interest
Ⓜ	nearest metro (underground) train station	❓	tours, lectures, or special events
🚆	nearest overground train station	▶	indicates the page where you will find a fuller description
		ℹ	tourist information

Citypack New York is divided into six sections to cover the six most important aspects of your visit to New York. It includes:

- The author's view of the city and its people
- Itineraries, walks and excursions
- The top 25 sights to visit – as selected by the author
- Features on what makes the city special
- Detailed listings of restaurants, hotels, shops and nightlife
- Practical information

In addition, easy-to-read side panels provide extra facts and snippets, highlights of places to visit, and invaluable practical advice.

CROSS-REFERENCES

To help you make the most of your visit, cross-references, indicated by ▶, show you where to find additional information about a place or subject.

MAPS

- **The fold-out map** in the wallet at the back of the book is a comprehensive street plan of New York. All the map references given in the book refer to this map. For example, the Chrysler Building, on Lexington Avenue, has the following information: ✚ E6 – indicating the grid square of the map in which the Chrysler Building will be found.
- **The city-centre maps** found on the inside front and back covers of the book itself are for quick reference. They show the Top 25 Sights, described on pages 24 – 48, which are clearly plotted by number (**1** – **25**, not page number) from south to north across the city.

PRICES

Where appropriate, an indication of the cost of an establishment is given by £ signs: £££ denotes higher prices, ££ denotes average prices, while £ denotes lower charges.

NEW YORK *life*

A PERSONAL VIEW

Vendors plying their trade on the city streets

What's that neighbourhood?

Almost every ten square blocks of Manhattan has a name.

Battery Park City
An official new neighbourhood, around the World Financial Center

Bowery
From Dutch farm (*bouwerie*) to skid row. Sleazy

Clinton
The city's uncatchy original name for Hell's Kitchen

Curry Hill & Row
Hill is E27th Street (Park/Lexington Avenues), Row is E6th Street (First/Second Avenues)

Diamond Row
Orthodox Hasidic Jews forge jewels here: W47th Street (Fifth/Sixth Avenues)

East Village
The name slapped on the tenements across town by bohemians priced out of Greenwich Village

Flatiron
A fairly recent recasting of the former photo district, and newish restaurants of Park Avenue South

Garment District
Where the 'garmentos' roam: 28th– 42nd Streets, round Seventh Avenue

Girl Ghetto
Cheap rent; east of Second Avenue, north of 68th Street

Your first sight of New York is like losing your virginity. Although you've heard so much about it and seen it in countless movies, you just don't get it until you've had the experience. Then, when you do finally find yourself in the middle of it, it's never what you expected.

I was lucky to have a great first time. Gotham was a humid, tropical 90-odd degrees when my friend picked me up at Kennedy and drove a midnight zigzag through Manhattan. All the sights – the skyline, the Empire State, Times Square, Fifth Avenue – were fantastic, but what thrilled me the most were the tall cylinders in the middle of roads belching out great ghostly clouds of steam. Nobody had ever mentioned those. The next day I fell in love with the friendly geometry of the ubiquitous fire escapes, and with the primitive silhouettes of water towers on roofs all over town.

Sometimes, I think of the early immigrants and how it was for them, especially those herded through Ellis Island, then crammed into Lower East Side tenements. I imagine how the cast-iron-framed SoHo buildings must have appeared to someone from, say, Vienna (like my father). Although now they're scenes of costly loft living, fancy interior stores and swank galleries, then they were sweatshop skyscrapers. They must have looked miraculous and more than a little daunting – symbols of hope for a fresh future; the immense energy of New York in concrete form.

Manhattan is built on a vortex magnetic to those who thrive on pace, change, adrenalin and, yes, chaos. We're dwarfed these days by the World Trade Center twin towers' 107 floors instead of the 'Cast Iron Historic District' of SoHo, which now appears human-sized. But New York's awe-inspiring first-time effect still works the same way – not through the big buildings, but through the lives inside them. It was really after that midnight car ride that I got my first taste of New York: the way everyone's in your face, and you have to interact with them; you have to deal. But, go figure, as they say here. Everyone knows, after the first time it gets a whole lot better.

The Manhattan skyline from the Empire State Building

Gramercy
Since the 1830s, when the Park was laid out

Greenwich Village
Probably the most famous neighbourhood of all

Hell's Kitchen
Midtown, way west. The name was coined late last century

Ladies' Mile
Big stores lined Broadway from Union to Madison Squares in the 19th century, hence this anachronism

Little Italy
Virtually reduced to one street: Mulberry, Spring to Canal

Murray Hill
Home to JP Morgan, and all 'the 400' – Lady Astor's crowd: 34th–42nd Streets, First–Fifth Avenues

NoHo
'North of Houston' – a few streets around Lafayette

SoHo
'South of Houston' was the first made-up name to stick

TriBeCa
The 'Triangle Below Canal' is all lofts and restaurants

Turtle Bay
Sutton and Beekman Place between 42nd and 59th Streets have been superexclusive since the 1920s

WeChe
West Chelsea is the newest 'nabe', way west in the 20s. We hope the name won't stick

NEW YORK IN FIGURES

DEMOGRAPHY
- Population New York City (NYC): 7.3 million
  (of which population Manhattan: 1.5 million)
- Average prison population: 18,736
- Catholic New Yorkers: 43.4 per cent
- Jewish New Yorkers: 10.9 per cent
- Baptist New Yorkers: 10.7 per cent
- Arrests in 1994: 89,000
- Murders in 1994: 517

GEOGRAPHY
- New York City area: 301sq miles
  (of which Manhattan area: 22.7sq miles;
  13.4 miles long by 0.8–2.3 miles wide)
- Miles of streets: 6,400
- Miles of subway track: 722
- Miles of waterfront: 578
- Acres of parks: 26,138
- Number of skyscrapers: 200
- Average annual rainfall: 47.25in
- Average annual snowfall: 29.3in

TOURISM
- Number of visitors in 1996: 30.3 million
- Number of airport passengers: 77.5 million
- Number of hotel rooms: 59,642
- Number of licensed taxis: 11,787
- Number of old chequered cabs: 8

LEISURE
- Number of restaurants: 17,000
- Number of art galleries: 400
- Number of Broadway theatres: 35
- Number of Off-Broadway theatres: 300
- Average Midtown traffic speed: 5.3mph
- 1995 rent for hot dog cart at Met: $316,200

Cab statistics

There is a fixed number of New York taxis, though with cab-driving being a traditional occupation of newly arrived immigrants the driver population changes constantly. In 1993, 1,694 new licences were granted – though not to the 29 per cent of applicants who failed the English proficiency test. At the last count, there were 85 different nationalities among New York taxi-drivers, with 60 languages spoken, but no guarantee of geographical fluency – the knowledge of Manhattan required is rudimentary.

NEW YORK PEOPLE

WOODY ALLEN

Since he has one of the world's best-known faces, it's very strange actually to see Woody, and you do see him, sooner or later. 'I can never leave,' he has said. Woody shares an unspoken pact with New Yorkers. Everyone knows not to stare at him, not at the Gramercy Tavern or Elaine's, not at a Knick's game at the Garden, not even when he's on stage on Mondays playing the clarinet at Michael's Pub. The Soon Yigate scandals of 1993 did remarkably little to taint the love his home town lavishes on the guy who made the neurotic, hypochondriac Upper East Side *mensch* into a world-wide cliché.

Woody Allen

DONNA KARAN

One of the few fashion designers to command movie-star-level recognition – at least of her name – Karan (emphasise the first syllable) came to fame well over a decade ago with a capsule collection of clothes for women over 20 based on a garment that has become the staple of every wardrobe, everywhere: the 'body'. Launching her 'DKNY' diffusion range widened the scope of this astute businesswoman and welded the idea of her clothes to the image of New York for ever, leading some to suggest that she pay royalties to the city. See her 20-storey mural at Broadway and Houston and decide for yourself.

DONALD TRUMP

You think you've heard the end of Donald, and then he starts up another scheme or marries another blonde. A former pet project, Trump Tower, the vulgar pink and gold block on Fifth Avenue, is pure frozen 1980s, but the 1990s are treating this highest-profile wheeler-dealer OK too, after a shaky start. The shaky start left him in debt to the tune of $8 billion, with $975 million of it personally guaranteed. Somehow, he came out with the Plaza Hotel (though Citicorp share the control), and his Taj Mahal gambling arena in Atlantic City, meanwhile divorcing Ivana and marrying Marla. Now he has the Trump International Hotel and Tower at Columbus Circle and is developing Riverside South.

New York types

Korean deli owner

It's impossible to envisage life before the Korean deli. Prices are ridiculously inflated, but it's a fair tax to pay on being able to get a banana-raisin-bran-nut muffin or a floor mop at 4AM.

Personal trainer

The gym boom is waning, as everyone journeys inwardly and does yoga and qigong, but this hasn't affected the 2:1 trainer-to-New Yorker ratio. A trainer is mentor, guru, scourge and saviour in one, and has been custom designed for NYC.

Panhandler

It's a very sad and unavoidable fact of life in the city that you will see more homeless people than you can count. Heavy competition for hardened New Yorkers' dimes leads to some irresistibly inventive lines.

9

A CHRONOLOGY

Pre-16th century	New York and the surrounding lands are populated by Native Americans
1524	Giovanni da Verrazano makes the first sighting of what is to be New York
1609	Henry Hudson sails up the Hudson seeking the North West Passage
1614	Adriaen Block names the area 'New Netherland'
1625	'Niew Amsterdam' is founded by the Dutch West India Company
1626	That colony's leader, Peter Minuit, buys Manhattan Island from the Indians for $24-worth of trinkets
1664	'Wall Street's' wall fails to deter the British, who invade and rename the island 'New York', after Charles II's brother, James, the Duke of York
1763	Treaty of Paris gives British control over 13 American colonies
1770	Battle of Golden Hill: Sons of Liberty vs the British
1774	New York 'Tea Party' – tax rebels empty an English tea clipper into New York harbour
1776	American Revolutionary War begins. British HQ in New York. Declaration of Independence read at Bowling Green in July
1783	Treaty of Paris ends war
1785	New York is named capital of the United States
1789	George Washington is sworn in as first US president at Federal Hall
1790	Philadelphia is named capital of the United States
1797	Albany takes over as capital of New York State

1807	Robert Fulton launches his first steamboat, which establishes trade routes along which many New Yorkers' fortunes lie
1827	Slavery in New York is abolished
1848	Start of first great immigrant waves
1861	Civil War. New York joins the Union cause
1868	The first 'El' – elevated railway – opens
1869	'Black Friday' on Wall Street
1886	The Statue of Liberty is unveiled
1892	Ellis Island opens
1904	The IRT line opens – New York's first subway
1929	The Stock Market crashes; the Great Depression begins
1930	Chrysler Building finished – world's tallest
1931	Empire State Building finished – world's tallest
1933	Prohibition ends. Fiorello La Guardia becomes mayor
1954	Ellis Island is closed down
1964	Race riots in Harlem and Brooklyn
1973	World Trade Center finished – world's tallest
1975	New York is bankrupt. Saved by federal loan
1980	John Lennon is murdered outside the Dakota
1987	Stock market crashes
1990	David Dinkins, New York's first black mayor, takes office
1993	Terrorist bomb damages the World Trade Center

PEOPLE & EVENTS FROM HISTORY

John Pierpont Morgan

John Pierpont Morgan

Banker J P Morgan (1837–1913) did everything with his money, from founding the Pierpont Morgan Library (► 55) to saving New York – in 1907 he and the US Treasury bought $25m of gold to rescue the city from bankruptcy. His millions derived from European investors in New York's 19th-century boomtime. He fielded those fortunes and watched over the founding of the US Steel Corporation.

TAMMANY HALL AND 'BOSS' TWEED

Tammany Hall was dedicated to fictional Iroquois chief 'St Tammany', in a spoof on the kind of upper-crust fraternities William Marcy 'Boss' Tweed and his cronies despised. A famous and typical Tweed extortion was the construction of the New York County Courthouse, which cost the city $14 million – $2 million for the building, and $12 million to line the pockets of the Tweed Ring. Bribery was routine for them. They bought votes with jobs and cash, and tried to buy – for $500,000 – the City Hall clerk who eventually shopped them. Tweed escaped from jail and fled, but was apprehended by Spanish police who recognised him from the Thomas Nast caricatures the *New York Times* had persisted in running. Altogether, the Tweed Ring defrauded New York of some $200 million.

NEW YORK FORTUNES

Certain names, enshrined in street names, foundations and cultural institutions, are inescapable in New York. Who were they?

John Jacob Astor (1763–1848) was a baddie. In 1834 he started investing the fortune he'd made in the fur trade in high-rent slums, squeezing pennies out of tenement dwellers while sucking up to high society. This made him the world's richest man at his death. The best thing he did was found the Public Library.

Andrew Carnegie (1835–1919) emigrated from Scotland, began as a cotton worker, and amassed vast fortunes through iron, coal and steel, ships and rail. Self-interest was not Carnegie's motivation. The $2 million for Carnegie Hall was the least of his gifts – libraries, trusts and charities benefited from his belief that to die rich is to die in disgrace.

Henry Clay Frick (1849–1919) ► 41.

Cornelius Vanderbilt (1794–1877) 'Commodore' Vanderbilt started with a ferry and ended with $105 million, which made him the richest American of his day. He converted the Staten Island Ferry into a steamship empire, then diversified into railways (► 36). After his death, son Cornelius (1843–99) doubled his money.

NEW YORK
how to organise your time

ITINERARIES

The best way to do New York is by not trying to see everything. You'll be so blinkered and exhausted, you'll miss what makes this a truly great city – things like the pace, the people, the chutzpah, the sights between the sights. In this spirit, the following itineraries are offered as guidelines for hanging a holiday on. If you do Itinerary Four on a Monday, Wednesday, Friday or Saturday, get off the bus at Union Square to pick up lunch from a Greenmarket stall (➤ 32). Saturday is ideal for visiting SoHo's galleries, although the Village will be swarming; avoid Sundays. For Itinerary Three, avoid Mondays as all the doors will be closed.

ITINERARY ONE	**LOWER MANHATTAN**
Morning	Ellis Island (➤ 26) Statue of Liberty (➤ 25) Brooklyn Bridge (➤ 29)
Lunchtime	Battery Park City (see panel opposite)
Afternoon	South Street Seaport (➤ 27) Walk through Financial District to:
Sunset	The World Trade Center (➤ 28) on West Side or Brooklyn Bridge on East Side
ITINERARY TWO	**MIDTOWN**
Morning	Museum of Modern Art (➤ 38) Rockefeller Center (➤ 37)
Lunchtime	Grand Central Terminal (➤ 36)
Afternoon	United Nations HQ (➤ 51) Walk through Midtown to Macy's (➤ 71)
Sunset	Empire State Building (➤ 33)
ITINERARY THREE	**MUSEUM MILE**
Morning	Metropolitan Museum of Art (➤ 44)
Lunchtime	Central Park (➤ 40)
Afternoon	Whitney Museum of American Art (➤ 42) Frick Collection (➤ 41)
Sunset	Across the Park to the Lincoln Center (➤ 39)

ITINERARY FOUR

UPTOWN–DOWNTOWN

Morning

Guggenheim Museum (► 45)
Cooper-Hewitt Museum of Design (► 46)

Lunchtime

Bus M1, 2, 3 or 18 down Fifth Avenue to
Astor Place

Afternoon

Greenwich Village (► 31)
Guggenheim SoHo, SoHo galleries, SoHo
shopping (► 45, 56 and 70)

The Empire State Building

Battery Park City

Battery Park City is still being
built on 92 acres of landfill along
the Hudson, and is due to be
finished around the turn of the
century. Cesar Pelli's World
Financial Center forms a part of it,
but you may care to explore the
residential areas of this futuristic
city-within-a-city, especially the
Esplanade (off Liberty Street) –
over a mile of waterside
promenade (or running track, as
you'll see), with fine views of the
harbour and New Jersey.

15

WALKS

INFORMATION

Distance 3 miles
Time 3 hours
Start point World Trade Center
🚇 A12
Ⓜ N, R, 1, 9 Cortlandt Street
End point Greenwich Village
🚇 B9
Ⓜ 1, 9 Christopher Street/
Sheridan Square

Brooklyn Bridge walkway

DOWNTOWN HIGHLIGHTS

Turn your back on the twin towers of the WTC, pass Century 21 department store to your left on Cortlandt Street, and head north up Broadway. As you approach City Hall Park on the right, look left just past Barclay Street for the Gothic 'Cathedral of Commerce', the Woolworth Building. Still on Broadway, City Hall and then the Tweed Courthouse come into view on your right.

Walk east through the park and catch a vista of Brooklyn Bridge. Continue north up Centre Street. You come to Cass Gilbert's gilt-pyramid-crowned US Courthouse on Foley Square at the south-east corner of Federal Plaza on your left, the neo-classical New York County Courthouse past Pearl Street on the right, then, past Hogan Street, the Criminal Courts (The Tombs).

A block further is gaudy Canal Street, which you follow east to Mulberry Street (for more of a taste of Chinatown, detour around this area). Continue north up this artery of Little Italy (you'll need an espresso – Caffe Roma on the corner of Broome Street is recommended), and veer west on Prince Street. After two blocks, you're in the Cast Iron Historic District of SoHo. Look at the Little Singer Building (above Kate's Paperie) opposite as you cross Broadway, reaching the SoHo Guggenheim on the right. Take any route you please west through the cobbled streets of SoHo from Mercer to MacDougal, at the same time heading north to cross Houston Street. Three blocks north along MacDougal, reach Washington Square, centre of New York University.

Fifth Avenue starts at the north side. Look at gated Washington Square Mews (first right), turn left on W8th Street (see MacDougal Alley, first left), and right onto Avenue of the Americas (Sixth Avenue). On the left is the crazily turreted Jefferson Market Library. Keep heading west and follow your nose (and page 31) to Greenwich Village, perhaps lunching at Mappamondo (✉ 11 Abingdon Square).

Live window display, Macy's

MIDTOWN'S GREATEST HITS

Madison Square Garden, behind Penn Station as you exit the subway, is not a garden at all, but a concrete cylinder for sports and concerts. Head two blocks uptown, then take 34th Street east one block to Herald Square, Macy's and Manhattan Mall. Toward the end of the next block, look up to your right. You're underneath the Empire State Building.

Head north up Fifth Avenue. Six blocks brings you to the *beaux-arts* magnificence of the New York Public Library, with Bryant Park behind. Go east on 42nd Street until you reach Grand Central Terminal; in the south-west corner of Park Avenue is the Whitney's outpost in the Philip Morris Building. After a look in the Terminal (the Oyster Bar or the café provides refreshment), continue east a block and a half and on the left you'll see the Chrysler Building. Circumnavigate the Terminal, hitting Park Avenue again at 46th Street, with the MetLife (Pan Am) building at your back.

A few blocks north you'll find the precursors of the Manhattan skyline: Lever House (north-west of 53rd Street) and Ludwig Mies van der Rohe's Seagram Building (east side, 52nd–53rd Streets). Go west on 53rd Street, south on Madison Avenue to 50th Street and veer west. Here's Saks Fifth Avenue and St Patrick's Cathedral, on the right. Straight ahead is the vast Rockefeller Center. If you have energy, the nearby Museum of Modern Art could wrap up your tour.

THE SIGHTS

- Madison Square Garden
- Macy's (➤ 71)
- Empire State Building (➤ 33)
- NY Public Library (➤ 34)
- Bryant Park (➤ 58)
- Whitney at Philip Morris (➤ 42)
- Grand Central Terminal (➤ 36)
- Chrysler Building (➤ 35)
- MetLife Building (➤ 51)
- Lever House, Seagram Building (➤ 51)
- St Patrick's Cathedral (➤ 52)
- Rockefeller Center (➤ 37)
- Museum of Modern Art (➤ 38)

INFORMATION

Distance 3 miles
Time 2 hours
Start point Madison Square Garden
- ✚ C7
- 🚇 1, 9 34th Street/Penn Station

End point Rockefeller Center
- ✚ E5
- 🚇 B, D, F 47th–50th Street/ Rockefeller Center

EVENING STROLLS

MUSEUM MILE – A STROLL DOWN FIFTH AVENUE

If it's summer, you may wish to start in the early evening – around 6PM – and add a Central Park preamble, using the entrance just north of the Met at 85th Street, and perhaps watching the competitive softball on the Great Lawn. Otherwise, start on Lexington Avenue at 96th Street, where, if it's dark, you may not wish to linger too long. Immediately you head west, however, the neighbourhood improves. This section of Park Avenue is called Carnegie Hill, and from here on this walk takes you through Manhattan's most expensive and desirable zip codes. When you reach Central Park, turn left down Fifth Avenue and just gaze at the fantastic façades, many of them still private homes. After another half-dozen blocks you reach the magnificent Metropolitan Museum of Art, then the Frick appears, followed by the fabulous Romanesque-Byzantine-style Temple Emanu-El ( 1 E65th Street), one of the world's largest synagogues and home of New York's oldest Reform congregation. Don't miss that round window.

THE EAST VILLAGE

Coming up from the subway on to the wasteland of Houston Street by Second Avenue is not an aesthetic experience, but as you take off north, you'll quickly get the feel of this land of the hip. On the right is Lucky Chengs (▶ 65), on the left Little Rickie's (▶ 77), followed by bars, restaurants, intriguing shops and boring stores. That block of 5th Street to the west is where exteriors for the NYPD Blue precinct are shot; the next block, 6th Street, is entirely filled with identical Indian restaurants with Christmas-light décor. St Mark's Place (8th Street) is the nerve centre of the neighbourhood. Go east one block to see the resurrected Tompkins Square Park, now surrounded by restaurants and bars (come back for a thorough exploration of Alphabet City – Avenues A to D were no-go areas not long ago). Go west all the way, and see how the punk funkiness gradually gives way to student pseudo-hipness, then to touristy fake coolness.

Park Avenue

ORGANISED SIGHTSEEING

A choice of tours The classic way to orientate yourself and get an eyeful of the skyline is to hop on a **Circle Line Cruise** (☎ 212/563 3200), which circumnavigates Manhattan for three hours, with commentary. Pricier, shorter, but more dramatic is a helicopter tour from **Island Helicopters** (☎ 212/683 4575), which scrapes the skyscrapers for between 7 and 35 miles. In between these extremes, slip the bus rides organised by **Gray Line** (☎ 212/397 2620), which include Trolley Tours on replicas of 1930s trolleys and many standard coach-ride-with-commentary orientation trips. **New York Doubledecker** (☎ 212/967 6008), meanwhile, ferries you around town in a transplanted London scarlet double-decker bus.

A Circle Line cruise boat

Walking tours Many of Seth Kamil and Ed O'Donnell's **Big Onion Walking Tours** (☎ 212/439 1090) are back-door gastronomic odysseys. But this entertaining duo also offer things like the 'Riot and Mayhem' tour of civil unrest sites. Another personalised, neighbourhood-crunching operation is **Adventure on a Shoestring** (☎ 212/265 2663), which has been leading small groups of walking tours for over 20 years. **'Wild Man' Steve Brill** (☎ 718/291 6825) leads the most surprising tours of all – around Manhattan's wilderness areas, with folkloric and ecological asides.

Cultural tours If you want insight into the arts, try one of several backstage tours. **Backstage on Broadway** (☎ 212/575 8065) has actors giving talks in daytime theatres, while the **Metropolitan Opera** (☎ 212/769 7020) and **Radio City Music Hall** (☎ 212/632 4041) both allow you into the workings. Some of the **Art Tours of Manhattan** (☎ 609/921 2647) and the **SoHo Art Tours** (☎ 212/431 8005) do a similar sort of thing with art, scheduling visits into the studios and lofts of actual artists. Also, the first crew will customise a visit to one of the major collections. **Literary Tours of Greenwich Village** (☎ 212/924 0239) retrace the steps of past authors, from Poe to Thomas.

EXCURSIONS

Brooklyn Heights

INFORMATION

Start point Grand Army Plaza
➕ Off map at G14
🚇 2, 3 Grand Army Plaza

Prospect Park
☎ Recorded info:
718/788 0055
♿ Good

Boathouse Visitor Center
🚇 D, Q Prospect Park
☎ 718/788 8549

Brooklyn Botanic Garden
✉ 1000 Washington Avenue
☎ 718/622 4433
🕐 Apr–Sep Tue–Fri 8–6;
weekends 10–6. Oct–Mar
Tue–Fri 8–4:30; weekends
10–4:30
🍴 Café
♿ Good
✋ Free

Brooklyn Museum
✉ 200 Eastern Parkway
☎ 718/638 5000
🕐 Wed–Sun 10–5
♿ Good
✋ Cheap

A BIT OF BROOKLYN
A separate city until 1898, this 71sq mile borough of well over 2 million souls is intimately connected to Manhattan, yet it is different – as even a superficial exploration proves.

Exit the subway at Grand Army Plaza, a vast oval traffic circus dominated by the Arc de Triomphe-like Soldiers' and Sailors' Arch, which functions as gateway to Prospect Park. Designers Olmsted and Vaux felt this park (opened in 1867) was better than their earlier Central Park. Inside is near-rural woodland and meadow, and the exquisite Brooklyn Botanic Garden with its Elizabethan Knot Garden, its Japanese Garden, its Conservatory and the Fragrance Garden with braille signs for the blind. Park Rangers give tours of the entire park, departing from the Boathouse.

On the park's north-east corner is the Brooklyn Museum. Intended by McKim, Mead & White to be the biggest museum in the world, it has turned out to be the seventh largest in the US, with collections from pre-Columbian (first floor) to 58 Rodin sculptures (fifth floor), and what's considered by many the best Egyptian collection outside the British Museum (and Egypt).

Of course, you shouldn't ignore the rest of Brooklyn, but it's a big place...For a flavour, stroll around leafy, middle-class Park Slope, north-west of the park, and around Brooklyn Heights south of the bridge – great Manhattan views.

STATEN ISLAND

Many Staten Islanders would like to secede from the city – why should they share New York's problems and taxes, they argue, when they not only have their own discrete, rather rural community, but are also completely ignored by all four other boroughs? Whatever their political status, however, their island is pure pleasure to visit, especially in summer when all manner of events are laid on. Once you've enjoyed the famous ferry ride, buses are the best way to get around.

Snug Harbor is a work in progress – a visual and performance arts centre in an 80-acre park of 28 historic buildings. Long established here are the Children's Museum and the Botanical Garden, as well as a couple of performance venues and a restored row of Greek Revival houses. Both this and historic Richmondtown have a programme of summer fairs, concerts and other events. In the dead centre of the island, Richmondtown traces 200 years of New York history through restored buildings, crafts workshops and costumed re-enactments. There's no better place to get a picture of how New York evolved.

A good use for a spare subway token is to take a ride on the Staten Island train, which takes about 40 minutes to travel its picturesque route from the ferry to Tottenville and includes a great view of the mighty Brooklyn-bound Verrazano-Narrows Bridge.

INFORMATION

➕ Off map at A14
🚢 Staten Island Ferry (➤ 53)

Snug Harbor Cultural Center
✉️ 1000 Richmond Terrace
☎️ 718/448 2500
🕐 8AM–dusk
🚌 $40
🍴 Melville's Café
♿ Good
🎫 Free

Richmondtown
✉️ 441 Clarke Avenue
☎️ 718/351 1611
🕐 Apr–Dec Wed–Sun 1–5.
   Jan–Mar Wed–Fri 1–5
🚌 $74
🍴 Tavern
♿ Moderate
🎫 Cheap

Snug Harbor

WHAT'S ON

For more information on events, see also pages 58, 60, 79 and 82.

JANUARY/FEBRUARY	*Chinese New Year parades*: ✉ Chinatown
MARCH	*St Patrick's Day Parade* (17 Mar): ✉ Fifth Avenue, 44th–86th Streets
MARCH/APRIL	*Easter Parade*: ✉ Fifth Avenue, 44th–59th Streets
APRIL	*Baseball season* starts (till Oct): ✉ Yankee and Shea stadiums
MAY	*Ninth Avenue International Food Festival*: ✉ Ninth Ave, 37th–57th Streets
	Martin Luther King Day Parade (3rd Sun): ✉ Fifth Ave, 44th–86th Streets
JUNE	*Metropolitan Opera parks concerts*: ☎ 212/362 6000
	JVC Jazz Festival: various venues ☎ 212/501 1390
	Lesbian and Gay Pride Parade: ☎ 212/463 9030
4 JULY	*Independence Day* (► 82)
JULY–AUGUST	*Shakespeare in the Park*: Delacorte Theater ☎ 212/539 8750
	NY Philharmonic parks concerts: ☎ 212/721 6500
AUGUST	*Harlem Week*: ☎ 212/427 7200
AUGUST–SEPTEMBER	*Lincoln Center Out-of-Doors Festival* (► 82): ☎ 212/875 5400
	US Open Tennis Championships: ☎ 718/760 6200
SEPTEMBER	*Feast of San Gennaro*: Little Italy
SEPTEMBER–OCTOBER	*New York Film Festival*: Lincoln Center ☎ 212/875 5050
OCTOBER	*Blessing of the Animals*: St John the Divine ☎ 212/316 7400
	Columbus Day Parade: ✉ Fifth Avenue, 44th–86th streets
	Hallowe'en Parade: Greenwich Village ☎ 914/758 5519
NOVEMBER	*NYC Marathon*: Verrazano-Narrows Bridge ☎ 212/860 4455
	Macy's Thanksgiving Day Parade: ☎ 212/494 5432
DECEMBER	*Tree Lighting Ceremony*: Rockefeller Center ☎ 212/632 3975
	New Year's Eve: Times Square, ball drops at midnight ☎ 212/768 1560

NEW YORK's
top 25 sights

*The sights are numbered from
south to north across the city*

CONEY ISLAND

INFORMATION

- Off map at A14
- Surf Avenue, Boardwalk, Brooklyn. Aquarium: W8th Street, Surf Avenue
- Aquarium: 718/265 3474
- Aquarium: daily 10–5; summer weekends and holidays 10–7
- Cafeteria at Aquarium
- B, D, F Stillwell Avenue/Coney Island, W8th Street, NY Aquarium
- B36, B68
- Good; aquarium very good
- Free; aquarium moderate

"Half slummy neighbourhood with the skeleton of a fairground, half sunny seaside resort with a peach of a boardwalk, Coney Island is redolent with other people's memories."

Nathan's and the Cyclone At the end of the last century, Coney Island on a peak day played host to a million people, attracted by Brooklyn's seaside air and by Luna Park, Dreamland and Steeplechase Park fairgrounds. By 1921, a boardwalk and the subway had joined the list of attractions, then the World's Fair of 1939–40 added the biggest draw of all, the 'Parachute jump'. At the end of this century, that machine is still there, a rusted ghost resembling a giant spider on stilts, and the glory days of Luna Park are long since gone, yet seedy Coney Island still draws a crowd. The big dipper ride the Cyclone is still there, more terrifying for the possibility of collapse than for the thrill of the ride (though it's not at all bad), and Nathan's Famous hot dogs are still sold from the original site, plus candy floss, saltwater taffy and corn dogs (franks deep fried in cornmeal).

Fish and freakshows The New York Aquarium, watery branch of the Bronx Zoo, moved here in 1957. Roughly 10,000 creatures call it home, including beluga whales, coral, a penguin colony and five varieties of shark. It's quite as wonderful as it sounds. The boardwalk Sideshow, though boasting an elastic lady and the blockhead (he hammers nails into his brain), is not the freak show it sounds, but a theatrical performance by East Village arty types.

The boardwalk along Brighton Beach, Coney Island

STATUE OF LIBERTY

❝*Not only does the green lady symbolise the American dream of freedom, but she quite takes your breath away, however many times you've seen her photograph – and despite her surprisingly modest stature.***❞**

How she grew In the late 1860s, sculptor Frédéric-Auguste Bartholdi dreamed of placing a monument to freedom in a prominent place. His dream merged with the French historian Edouard-René de Laboulaye's idea of presenting the American people with a statue celebrating freedom and the two nations' friendship. Part of the idea was to shame the repressive French government, but, apparently, New Yorkers took their freedom for granted, and it was only after Joseph Pullitzer promised to print the name of every donor in his newspaper, the *New York World*, that the city's ordinary citizens coughed up the funds to build the statue's pedestal. She was finally unveiled by President Grover Cleveland on 28 October 1886 in a ceremony from which women were banned.

Mother of exiles Emma Lazarus's stirring poem, *The New Colossus*, is engraved on the pedestal, while the tablet reads: July IV MDCCLXXVI – the date of the Declaration of Independence. Beneath her size 107 feet, she tramples the broken shackles of tyranny, and her seven-pointed crown beams liberty to the seven continents and the seven seas.

What is she made of? Gustave Eiffel practised for his later work by designing the 1,700-bar iron and steel structure that supports her. She weighs 225 tons, is 151ft tall, has an 8ft index finger and has a skin of 300 copper plates. The torch tip towers 305ft above sea level.

HIGHLIGHTS

- The climb to the crown
- The view from the pedestal
- Statue of Liberty Museum
- Fort Wood, the star-shaped pedestal base
- Her new centenary flame

INFORMATION

- ➕ Off map at A14
- ✉ Liberty Island
- ☎ 212/363 3200. Ferry: 212/269 5755. Ticket office: 212/344 7220
- 🕐 Jul–Aug daily 9–6; Sep–Jun daily 9:30–5. Closed 25 Dec
- 🍴 Cafeteria
- 🚇 1, 9 South Ferry; 4, 5 Bowling Green; N, R Whitehall Street
- 🚌 M1, M6, M15 South Ferry
- ⛴ Ferry departs Battery Park South Ferry (A13). Tickets from Castle Clinton National Monument, Battery Park
- ♿ Few
- 💷 Cheap
- ↔ Battery Park City (➤ 15), Ellis Island (➤ 26) (joint admission), Staten Island Ferry (➤ 53)
- ❓ Audio tours available

3

ELLIS ISLAND

INFORMATION

- Off map at A14
- Ellis Island
- 212/363 3200
- Jul–Aug daily 9–6;
  Sep–Jun daily 9:30–5.
  Closed 25 Dec
- Café
- 1, 9 South Ferry;
  4, 5 Bowling Green;
  N, R Whitehall Street
- M1, M6, M15
- Ferry departs Battery Park
  South Ferry (A13). Tickets
  from Castle Clinton National
  Monument, Battery Park
- Good
- Cheap
- Battery Park City (▶ 15),
  Statue of Liberty (▶ 25;
  joint admission), Staten
  Island Ferry (▶ 53)
- Audio tours available

One of the city's newer museums offers the near-compulsory humbling taste of how the huddled masses of new immigrants were not allowed to go free until they'd been herded through these halls, weighed, measured and rubber stamped.

Half of all America It was the poor who docked at Ellis Island after sometimes gruelling voyages in steerage, since first-class passage included permission to decant straight into Manhattan. Annie Moore, aged 15 and the first immigrant to disembark here, arrived in 1892, followed by 16 million founding fathers over the next 40 years, including such American-sounding Americans as Irving Berlin and Frank Capra. Half the population of the United States can trace their roots to an Ellis Island immigrant.

Island of tears The exhibition in the main building conveys the indignities, frustrations and, above all, fears of the arrivals. (As soon as you arrive, collect your free ticket for the half-hour film, *Island of Hope/Island of Tears*, which you'll otherwise end up missing.) You are guided around more or less the same route the millions took: from the Baggage Room, where they had to abandon all they owned; on to the enormous Registry Room, now bare not only of people, but of furniture too; and on through the series of inspection chambers where medical, mental and political status were ascertained. The Oral History Studio brings it all to life as immigrants recount their experience – especially moving when coupled with the poignant possessions in the 'Treasures from Home' exhibit. All this makes for a demanding few hours' sightseeing, which you'll probably be combining with the Statue of Liberty, since the ferries stop at both islands. Wear sensible shoes; bring lunch.

Top: the Ellis Island National Monument

SOUTH STREET SEAPORT

❝*This reconstructed historic maritime district, with its cobbled streets, is something of a tourist trap. However, when you stroll the boardwalk on a summer's night, with the moon over the East River, you are quite glad to be a tourist.***❞**

Pier, cruise, shop, eat The seaside/cruise-ship atmosphere is what's fun at the Pier 17 Pavilion,

The Seaport in the evening

which juts 400ft into the East River, overlooking Brooklyn Heights. It's a mall, with chain stores, bad restaurants and a Food Court, but also three storeys of charming wooden decks. The adjoining piers, 16 and 15, harbour a number of historic vessels with picturesque arrangements of rigging, plus the replica sidewheeler, *Andrew Fletcher*, and the 1885 schooner, *Pioneer*, which give harbour cruises. On land, your cash is courted by many shops, housed in the 1812 Federal-style warehouses of Schermerhorn Row – Manhattan's oldest block – and around Water, Front and Fulton Streets, and also by the few remaining cafés in the old Fulton Market.

Many museums The Seaport Museum Visitors' Center acts as clearing house for all the small-scale exhibitions here. One ticket admits you to the second-biggest sailing ship ever built, the *Peking*; the floating lighthouse, *Ambrose*; the Children's Center; the Seaport Museum Gallery, a re-creation of a 19th-century printer's shop; various walking tours; and more.

HIGHLIGHTS

- The view of Brooklyn Heights
- Richard Haas' Brooklyn Bridge mural
- Late-night forays in the Fulton Fish Market (midnight–8AM)
- Boarding *Andrew Fletcher*
- Watching the Wall Street young decant into the bars around 5PM
- The *Titanic* Memorial
- The Chandlery
- Fulton Market (especially the bakeries)
- The incongruous giant bubble (tennis courts!)
- The sea breeze

INFORMATION

- ✛ B12/13
- ✉ Visitor Center, 12 Fulton Street; tickets also from Pier 16
- ☎ 212/669 9424
- 🕐 Jun–Sep Fri–Wed 10–6; Oct–May Fri–Wed 10–5. Closed 25 Dec, 1 Jan
- 🍴 Too numerous to list
- 🚇 2, 3, 4, 5, J, M, Z Fulton Street; A, C Broadway/Nassau Street
- 🚌 M15 Pearl/Fulton Street
- ♿ Few/none
- 💲 Free–moderate
- ↔ World Trade Center (► 28), Brooklyn Bridge (► 29)
- ❓ Walking tours: 'Ship Restoration', 'Back Streets', etc

5

WORLD TRADE CENTER

INFORMATION

- ✛ A12
- ✉ World Trade Center, between Liberty and Vesey streets
- 🕐 Jun–Sep daily 9:30AM–11:30PM. Oct–May daily 9:30–9:30
- 🍴 Windows on the World ☎ 212/938 1111. Cellar in the Sky ☎ 212/524 7000
- 🚇 C, E World Trade Center; 1, 9, N, R Cortlandt Street
- 🚌 M10
- 🚆 PATH WTC
- ♿ Good
- 🎫 Cheap–moderate
- ↔ Battery Park City (➤ 15), World Financial Center (➤ 51)

❝Not much liked when they went up (and up and up) in the 1970s, the Twin Towers practically define the lower Manhattan skyline. Four boring buildings, the Vista hotel and a mall complete the Center, but the view is the point. **❞**

Scary skyscrapers The twin towers are like jellyfish in that their outer covering is all that holds them together. Minoru Yamasaki's design replaced the steel skeleton of the average skyscraper with load-bearing exterior walls of vertical columns and gigantic horizontal spandrel beams. Large windows for the workers' warren inside were sacrificed. The workers themselves were nearly sacrificed in February 1993, when a terrorist bomb rocked Floor 1 WTC.

Vital statistics The towers' 110 floors rise 1,350ft, supplying 10 million sq ft of office space for 50,000 workers. Each tower contains 99 elevators, but the 80,000 daily visitors are allocated a single express that reaches the 107th floor of Tower Two in 58 seconds flat. Although over 1,000 people were injured in the 1993 bomb blast, the walls ran red not with blood, but with wine – over $2 million worth of bottles were blasted from the Cellar in the Sky, now reopened and serving a seven-course *prix-fixe* menu.

No vertigo After they were finished in 1973, the towers attracted aerial mayhem. Philippe Petit walked a towertop-to-towertop tightrope in August 1974, for which he was arrested and ordered to do kids' shows in Central Park. A year later, Owen Quinn parachuted off the top. Recklessness charges were dropped. Finally, in May 1977, George Willig, using crampons of his own design, climbed up a tower. The city sued for $250,000, but accepted $1.10.

BROOKLYN BRIDGE

❝ *The view from the Bridge is spectacular, but the structure itself, with its twin Gothic towers and ballet of cables, means the first Manhattan–Brooklyn link fulfils beautifully its symbolic role of affording entry into new worlds of opportunity.* **❞**

Killer bridge In 1869, before construction had even started, the original engineer, John Roebling, had his foot crushed by a ferry and died of gangrene three weeks later. His son, Washington, took over the project, only to succumb to the bends and subsequent paralysis. Washington's wife, Emily Warren, finished overseeing the construction, during which 20 workmen died in various nasty accidents. Then, on 30 May 1883, a few days after the opening, a woman fell over, screamed and set off a 20,000-person stampede, which claimed 12 more lives. Robert Odlum's was the first non-accidental Bridge-related death. He jumped off for a bet in 1885 and subsequently died from internal bleeding.

Bridge of sighs Now, the occasional leaper chooses the cable walk as their last, but things are mostly peaceful. The best time and direction to walk the footpath is east from Brooklyn to Manhattan at dusk. The sun sets behind Liberty Island and, as you stroll on, Downtown looms larger and larger, the sky darkens to cobalt, the lights go on, the skyline goes sparkly, and you are swallowed into the metropolis. It's a transcendental half-hour. Although you'll almost certainly be fine, it's still not a good plan to walk over the bridge at night, especially carrying cameras. And keep to the uptown side; the other lane is for bikes.

HIGHLIGHTS

- The walk to Manhattan
- The panorama of NY buildings
- The cables – each consisting of 5,282 wires
- Jehovah's Witnesses' *Watchtower* HQ
- Cars hurtling, 6yds below your feet
- Cyclists hurtling, 6in from your face

INFORMATION

- ✚ C13
- ✉ Walkway entrance is across Park Row from City Hall Park
- Ⓢ 4, 5, 6 Brooklyn Bridge/City Hall; J, M, Z Chambers Street
- 🚌 M1, M6
- ♿ Very good
- 🎟 Free
- ↔ South Street Seaport (▶ 27)

The Lower Manhattan skyline from beneath Brooklyn Bridge

CHINATOWN

HIGHLIGHTS

- Buddhist temple (✉ 64B Mott Street)
- Chinatown History Museum (✉ 70 Mulberry Street)
- Pearl River Mart (✉ 277 Canal Street)
- Doyers Street: once the 'Bloody Angle'
- Chinatown Ice Cream Factory (✉ 65 Bayard Street)
- Columbus Park (✉ Bayard/Baxter Streets)
- The Tombs, or Criminal Courts Building (✉ 100 Centre Street)
- Cecilia Tam's egg cakes (✉ Mosco/Mott Streets)

INFORMATION

- ✚ C11/12
- ✉ Roughly delineated by Worth Street/East Broadway, the Bowery, Grand Street and Centre Street
- ⊙ Some restaurants close around 10PM
- ⑪ About 350
- ⊟ J, M, Z, N, R, 6, A, C, E, 1, 9 Canal Street; B, D Grand Street
- ⊟ M1, B51
- ⚭ None
- ⟷ SoHo Guggenheim (➤ 45), Little Italy (➤ 54), Lower East Side Tenement Museum (➤ 55)
- ❓ General tours: ☎ 212/619 4785. Chinese herbal medicine tours: ☎ 212/219 2527

"New York's Chinatown, the largest in the West, encroaches on what remains of Little Italy and the Jewish Lower East Side, even on Hispanic 'Loisaida'. Wander here, and you're humbled by the sight of a lifestyle which, making no concessions to the visitor, remains for ever opaque."

Going west Prefiguring the movement of emigrants from the devolved Russia and Eastern Europe of today, Chinese people first came to New York in the late 19th century, looking to work a while, make some money and return home. But, by 1880 or so, some 10,000 men – mostly Cantonese railroad workers decamped from California – had become stranded between Canal, Worth and Baxter Streets. Tongs (a sort of secret mafia operation, similar to the Triads) were formed, and still keep order today over some 150,000 Chinese, Taiwanese, Vietnamese, Burmese and Singaporeans. New York, incidentally, has two more Chinatowns: in Flushing, Queens, and Eighth Avenue, Brooklyn, with a further 150,000-odd inhabitants.

A closed world Although you may happily wander its colourful, slightly manic streets, you will never penetrate Chinatown. Many of its denizens never learn English, never leave its environs, never have left its environs and never wish to. The 600 factories and 350 restaurants keep them in work, then there are the tea shops, mah-jong parlours, herbalists and fishmongers. Chinatown also has the highest bank-to-citizen ratio in New York, in which Chinese stash their wages (normally not more than $10,000–$20,000 a year) to save for the 'eight bigs' (car, TV, video recorder, fridge, camera, phone, washing machine and furniture), to send home, or eventually to invest in a business of their own.

GREENWICH VILLAGE

"This toothachingly picturesque, human-scale neighbourhood of brownstones and actual trees is the other romantic image of Manhattan (second to the skyline), familiar from sitcoms and movies. Its dense streets are rewarding to wander."

What village? It was named after Greenwich, southeast London, by the British colonists who settled here at the end of the 17th century. The 18th and early 19th centuries saw the wealthy founders of New York society taking refuge here from smallpox, cholera and yellow fever.

Bohemia, academe, jazz When the élite moved on and up, the bohemian invasion began, pioneered by Edgar Allan Poe, who moved to 85 W3rd Street in 1845. Fellow literary habitués included Mark Twain, O Henry, Walt Whitman, F Scott Fitzgerald, Eugene O'Neill, John Dos Passos and ee cummings. New York University arrived in Washington Square in 1831 and grew into the country's largest private university. Post World War II, bohemia became beatnik; a group of abstract artists centred around Jackson Pollock, Mark Rothko and Willem de Kooning also found a home here.

Freedom parades Café Society, where Billie Holiday made her 1938 début, was one of the first non-racially segregated clubs in New York. Thirty years later, a different kind of discrimination was challenged, when police raided the Stonewall Inn on 28 June 1969, arresting gay men for illegally buying drinks and setting off the Stonewall Riots – the birth of the Gay Rights Movement. The Inn stood on Christopher Street, which became the main drag (no pun intended) of New York's gay community and ranked with San Francisco for excitement.

HIGHLIGHTS

- Cafés and jazz clubs
- Washington Square Park
- NYC's narrowest house (✉ 75 Bedford Street)
- The West (of Hudson Street) Village
- The Hallowe'en Parade (31 Oct)
- Jefferson Market Library
- Balducci's (the grocers)
- Minetta Lane
- Carmine Street pool (Clarkson Avenue/Seventh Avenue South)

Washington Memorial Arch

INFORMATION

✚	B9–C9
✉	East to west from Broadway to Hudson Street; north to south from 14th Street to Houston Street
🍴	Thousands
Ⓜ	A, C, E, B, D, F W4th Street; 1, 9 Christopher Street
🚌	M10
🚇	PATH Christopher Street
♿	None
↔	SoHo (▶ 54)

31

9

UNION SQUARE

HIGHLIGHTS

- The Saturday Greenmarket
- Union Square Café
- Models posing in The Coffee Shop
- The Amish Farms stall
- The Pretzel Man
- Jazz at Metropolis Café
- Toys 'R' Us and Bradlees
- American Savings Bank Building
- The seafood stall
- Apple season

INFORMATION

- ✚ D9
- ✉ W14th–17th Streets, Park Avenue South, Broadway
- ☎ Greenmarket: 212/788 7900
- 🕙 Greenmarket: Mon, Wed, Fri, Sat 8–6
- 🍴 Numerous
- 🚇 4, 5, 6, L, N, R 14th Street, Union Square
- 🚌 M3
- ♿ Few

"For proof that New York evolves constantly, see Union Square. A needle park in the 1970s, it's now where downtown meets uptown, with fabulous foodie restaurants, a wild café scene and the egalitarian highlight of all Manhattan: the Greenmarket."

Not those Unions Laid out in 1839, Union Square had close encounters with socialism though its name actually refers to the union of Broadway and Fourth Avenue. It was a mecca for soapbox orators in the first three decades of this century, then, during the 1930 Depression, 35,000 unemployed rallied here *en route* to City Hall to demand work; workers' May Day celebrations convened here, too. Later, Andy Warhol picked up on the vibes, set up his Factory (in the south-west corner), and began publishing his style mag, *Interview*, where once the *Daily Worker* had been produced.

Green In summer, the park teems with office refugees, sharing the lawn with an equestrian George Washington, by John Quincy Adams Ward, an Abe Lincoln, by Henry Kirke Brown, and a Marquis de Lafayette, which Frédéric-Auguste Bartholdi, of subsequent Statue of Liberty fame, gave the city in 1876. Mondays, Wednesdays, Fridays and Saturdays are Greenmarket days. An entire culture, an actual Manhattan lifestyle, has grown around this collation of stalls overflowing with home-grown and home-made produce from New England farmers and fishers and bakers and growers. Everyone has their favourite farmer. Cult highlights include: the maple candies, the Amish cheeses, the Pretzel Man (and his pretzels), the fresh clams, the sugar-free muffins and the hundred blends of mesclun salad. Curiously, the Square also harbours some of the city's tackiest superstores.

Top: the Saturday market in Union Square

EMPIRE STATE BUILDING

❝It was not Fay Wray's fault, nor Cary Grant's in An Affair to Remember, *that this is the most famous skyscraper in the world. Rather, its fame is the reason that it has appeared in every New York movie. You have to climb it.❞*

King for 40 years The Empire State Building is the very definition of 'skyscraper', and it was the highest man-made thing until the World Trade Center went up in the 1970s. Construction began in 1929, not long before the great Wall Street Crash, and by the time it was topped in 1931 – construction went at the superfast rate of four storeys a week – so few could afford to rent space that they called it 'the Empty State Building'. Only the popularity of its observatories kept the wolves from the door. These viewpoints still attract around 35,000 visitors a day. Many stop off on the Mezzanine for the newest attraction, the New York Skyride, which simulates a rooftop flight, including a hair-raising virtual crash over Wall Street; the tour guide is James Doohan – *Star Trek*'s 'Scottie'.

The numbers It is 1,250ft high, and there are 102 floors. The frame contains 60,000 tons of steel, 10 million bricks line the building, and there are 6,500 windows taking up 5 acres. The speediest of the 73 elevators climb 1,200ft per minute. The speediest runners in the annual Empire State Run-Up climb almost 170 steps per minute, making the 1,860 steps to the 102nd floor in 11 minutes, though average people take about half an hour just to climb down! It is not necessarily worth the (up to 60-minute) wait to climb the extra 16 floors to the glass-encased 102nd floor.

HIGHLIGHTS

- The view: by day, at dusk and by night
- The view up from 34th Street
- New York Skyride
- Penny-flattening machine
- The lights on the top 30 storeys (4 July, Hallowe'en and Christmas)

INFORMATION

- ✚ D7
- ✉ 350 Fifth Avenue, W34th Street
- ☎ 212/736 3100
- ◷ Daily 9:30AM–midnight. Last admission 11:30PM
- ⌘ Snack bar
- Ⓢ B, D, F, N, R 34th Street
- 🚌 M1, M2, M3, M4, M5, M16, M34
- 🚉 PATH 33rd Street
- ♿ Good
- 💲 Cheap
- ↔ NY Public Library (▶ 34), Chrysler Building (▶ 35), Macy's (▶ 71)

Top: the view
Below: the entrance hall

11

NEW YORK PUBLIC LIBRARY

HIGHLIGHTS

- Patience and Fortitude
- Truth and Beauty
- T S Eliot's typed *The Waste Land*
- Jefferson's handwritten Declaration of Independence
- Astor Hall
- The shop
- Thomas Hastings' flagpost bases
- Gottesman Hall ceiling

INFORMATION

- D6
- 476 Fifth Avenue (42nd Street)
- 212/869 8089
- Thu–Sat 10–6; Tue–Wed 11–7:30. Closed holidays
- Kiosks outside (not winter)
- 4, 5, 6, 7, S 42 Street Grand Central
- M101, M102
- Metro North, Grand Central
- Good (see also below)
- Free
- Empire State Building (➤ 33), Chrysler Building (➤ 35), Grand Central Terminal (➤ 36), Bryant Park (➤ 58)
- Tours: 11AM and 2PM daily Notable branches include: the Andrew Heiskell Library for the Blind and Physically Handicapped (✉ 40 W20th Street) and the Library for the Performing Arts (✉ 40 Lincoln Plaza)

"Why are we sending you to a library on your holidays? Because the NY Public Library's Central Research Building is a great, white, hushed palace, quite beautiful to behold even if you have no time to open a book."

The building Carrère and Hastings (who also designed the Frick, ➤ 41) were the architects responsible for what is generally thought to be the city's best representative of the *beaux-arts* style – the sumptuous yet classical French school that flourished in New York's 'gilded age': about 1880–1920. A pair of lions, which Mayor La Guardia christened Patience and Fortitude, flank the majestic stair that leads directly into the barrel-vaulted, carved white marble temple of Astor Hall. The lions are themselves flanked by fountains, 'Truth' and 'Beauty', which echo the site's previous (1845–99) incarnation as the Croton Reservoir supplying the city's water. Behind this briefly stood New York's version of London's Crystal Palace, built for the first American World's Fair in 1853. Like the London one, it burned down. Inside, see temporary exhibitions in the Gottesman Hall, and look up! The carved oak ceiling is sublime. Read in the two-block-long Main Reading Room, see library collection rarities in the Salomon Room, and don't miss the Richard Haas murals of NYC publishing houses in the De Witt Wallace Periodical Room.

The books The Library owns over 15 million books, most of which are kept in the 82 branches. This building is dedicated to research. The CATNYP computer, complete with dumb waiter, can disgorge any of the 16 million manuscripts or 3 million books from the 92 miles of stacks in just ten minutes flat.

Top: the reading room

CHRYSLER BUILDING

> **'Which is your favourite New York building?'** goes the annoying yet perennial question. As it turns out, nine out of ten people who express a preference choose the Chrysler Building over other brands. This should surprise no one who gazes on it.

King for a year The tower, commissioned from William Van Alen by Walter Chrysler (who asked for something 'taller than the Eiffel Tower'), won the world's tallest building competition in 1930...until the Empire State Building went up the following year. Van Alen had been almost pipped to the post by Craig Severance's Bank of Manhattan tower at 40 Wall Street, when his rival, aware of the unofficial race, slung on an extra 2ft. Unbeknownst to Severance, though, Van Alen was secretly constructing a 123ft stainless-steel spire, which he 'posted' out through the 925ft roof, beating the 927-footer hands down. It's ironic that the best view of the art deco beauty's top is now gained from the observatory at the Empire State.

Multi-storey car Every detail of the 77-storey building evokes the motor car – a 1929 Chrysler Plymouth, to be exact. The winged steel gargoyles are modelled on its radiator caps; other of the building's stepped setbacks carry stylised hubcaps, and the entire spire resembles a radiator grille; and this ain't no Toyota. The golden age of motoring is further evoked by the stunning lobby, which you can visit – ostensibly to view the Con Edison (New York's utilities company) conservation exhibit, but really to see the red marble, granite and chrome interior, surmounted by the 97ft by 100ft mural depicting industrial scenes and celebrating 'transportation'.

HIGHLIGHTS

- The spire
- The ceiling mural
- The elevator cabs
- The fourth setback gargoyles
- The African marble lobby

INFORMATION

- ✚ E6
- ✉ 405 Lexington Avenue (42nd Street)
- 🕐 Mon–Fri 7AM–6PM. Closed holidays
- Ⓢ 4, 5, 6, 7, S 42nd Street, Grand Central
- 🚌 M101, M102
- 🚉 Metro North, Grand Central
- ♿ Good
- 🎟 Free
- ↔ Empire State Building (➤ 33)

The pinnacle of success

35

GRAND CENTRAL TERMINAL

HIGHLIGHTS

- The Main Concourse ceiling
- The Oyster Bar
- The bar over the Main Concourse
- Mercury on the 42nd Street façade
- The clock
- The free art installations
- The 75ft arched windows
- The Grand Staircase
- The uneven Tennessee marble floor
- Municipal Arts Society tours

INFORMATION

- ✚ E6
- ✉ Park Avenue (42nd Street)
- ☎ 212/532 4900
- 🕐 5:30AM–1:30AM daily
- 🍴 Restaurant, café/bar, snack bars
- 🚇 4, 5, 6, 7, S 42nd Street, Grand Central
- 🚌 M101, 102 Grand Central
- 🚆 Metro North, Grand Central
- ♿ Good
- 🎫 Free
- ↔ Empire State Building (► 33), NY Public Library (► 34), Chrysler Building (► 35), Bryant Park (► 58)
- ❓ Tours: Wed 12.30PM. Meet by Chemical Bank in Main Concourse

"Don't call it a station. All tracks terminate here, which makes this railway mecca a far grander entity. The beaux-arts building bustles like no place else; stand here long enough, and the entire world passes by."

Heart of the nation 'Grand Central Station!' bellowed (erroneously) the 1937 opening of the eponymous NBC radio drama; 'Beneath the glitter and swank of Park Avenue… Crossroads of a million private lives!… Heart of the nation's greatest city…'. And so it is, and has been since 1871 when the first, undersized version was opened by Commodore Cornelius Vanderbilt, who had bought up all the city's railroads just like on a giant Monopoly board. See him in bronze below Jules-Alexis Coutans' allegorical statuary on the main (south, 42nd Street) façade. The current building dates from 1913 and is another *beaux-arts* glory, its design modelled partly on the Paris Opéra by architects Warren and Wetmore. William Wilgus was the logician responsible for traffic-marshalling, while Reed and Stem were the overall engineers. Recent cleaning of the Main Concourse ceiling has re-revealed the stunning sight of 2,500 'stars' in a cerulean sky, with medieval-style zodiac signs by French artist Paul Helleu.

Meeting under the clock The fame of the four-faced clock atop the information booth is out of all proportion to its size. (You may remember the scene in the movie *The Fisher King* where thousands of commuters fell into synchronised waltzing around it.) Beneath the clock, and the ground, is a warren of 32 miles of tracks, tunnels and vaulted chambers, in one of which the famed Oyster Bar resides. Be careful what you say here – it's like being in a whispering gallery.

ROCKEFELLER CENTER

❝This small village of famous art deco buildings provides many of those 'gee this is New York' moments: in winter when you see ice-skaters ringed by the flags of the UN, or anytime over cocktails in the Rainbow Room.**❞**

Prometheus is here The buildings' bible, Willensky and White's *AIA Guide to NYC*, calls the 19-building Rockefeller Center: 'The greatest urban complex of the 20th century.' It is 'the heart of New York,' agreed the Landmarks Commission in 1985. So the architectural importance of the Center – and especially the elongated ziggurat GE Building (better known as the RCA Building) – is beyond dispute, but it's still easy to enjoy the place. Rest on a Channel Gardens bench, enjoy the seasonal foliage, and gaze on the lower plaza, the rink and Paul Manship's *Prometheus*. The Channel is a reference to the English Channel, since these sloping gardens separate La Maison Française from the British Empire Building.

Rockefeller the Younger The realisation of John D Rockefeller Jr's grand scheme to outdo dad (Mister Standard Oil) provided work for a quarter of a million souls during the Depression. In 1957, Marilyn Monroe detonated the dynamite for the Time & Life buildings' foundations, and the Center was still growing into the 1970s.

Conan and Rockettes For many years, the NBC Studios in the GE Building hosted the hip TV talk show *Late Night* with David Letterman. Dave decamped to CBS (where he lost all cool), and Conan O'Brian was plucked from obscurity to host the spot. Over on Avenue of the Americas is Radio City Music Hall, landmark home to the Rockettes, born in 1934 and still kicking.

Atlas, *Lee Lawrie*

HIGHLIGHTS

- The GE Building, outside
- The GE Building's lobbies
- The Rainbow Room
- NBC Studio tour
- Skating in winter
- The Sea Grill restaurant
- Radio City Music Hall
- Channel Gardens
- *Prometheus*
- Atlas (Fifth Avenue, 50th–51st Street)

INFORMATION

- ✚ E5
- ✉ Fifth–Seventh Avenues (47th–52nd Streets)
- 🕐 Various hours
- 🍴 Numerous restaurants, cafés
- Ⓜ B, D, F 47–50th Streets, Rockefeller Center
- 🚌 M1, M2, M3, M4, M5, M18
- ♿ Varies
- 🎟 Free
- ↔ MoMA (➤ 38)
- ❓ Radio City tours: ☎ 212/ 632 4041. NBC Studio tours: ☎ 212/664 4000

15

MUSEUM OF MODERN ART

HIGHLIGHTS

- *Water Lilies*, Monet
- *Dance*, Matisse
- *Les Demoiselles d'Avignon*, Picasso
- *Starry Night*, Van Gogh
- *Broadway Boogie-Woogie*, Mondrian
- *The Persistence of Memory*, Dali
- *One*, Pollock
- *Flag*, Jasper Johns
- *Gold Marilyn Monroe*, Warhol
- The film programme

INFORMATION

- E5
- 11 W53rd Street
- 212/708 7500
- Fri–Tue 11–6; Thu 11–9. Closed 25 Dec
- Restaurant
- B, D, E Seventh Avenue; E, F Fifth Avenue
- M5, M6, M7, M18
- Few
- Moderate

MoMA's modern façade

"*A great collection housed in a cool building – literally in summer. The film programme is practically the final fling of repertory cinema in New York; even the shop and the popular restaurant are modern and arty.***"**

Van Gogh to Man Ray Founded on the 1931 bequest of Lillie P Bliss, which consisted of 235 works, the MoMA collections now amount to about 100,000 pieces of art. True to the museum's title, these include modern arts: photography, graphic design, household objects, conceptual art and industrial design, though work from the first half of the century is better represented than the really new – go to the Whitney for that. There are four floors, plus the Abby Aldrich Rockefeller Sculpture Garden – where you can retreat from the city in the company of Rodin, Picasso and Moore. The works are arranged more or less chronologically, with temporary shows sharing the upper floors with architecture and design.

Post-Impressionists to Graffiti artists The collection starts in the late 19th century, with the Post-Impressionists and Fauvists: Cézanne, Van Gogh (pronounced 'van go' round here), Seurat, Gauguin and Matisse. Most movements of this century follow – Cubism, Expressionism, Futurism, Surrealism, Abstract Expressionism – up to and including Pop (Oldenburg, Dine, Rauschenberg, Warhol, of course), and the 'Graffiti' work of Keith Haring and Jean-Michel Basquiat. What was probably MoMA's most famous and important painting of all no longer hangs here. It was Picasso's 1937 *Guernica*, which, post-Franco, was given back to the Spanish.

LINCOLN CENTER

"Strolling to the fantastically fairy-lit ten-storey Metropolitan Opera House colonnade across the Central Plaza on a winter's night is one of the most glamorous things you can do on this earth, and you don't need tickets."

West Side Story The ambitious Rockefeller-funded über-arts centre was envisaged in the late 1950s and finished in 1969, after 7,000 families and 800 businesses had been turfed out of their homes by developer Robert Moses and the John D Rockefeller millions. Much of *West Side Story* was actually shot on these streets after the demolition had begun, capturing the pain of change for ever.

All the arts The 15 acres include megahouses for the biggest-scale arts, all designed by different architects in the same white travertine. The Metropolitan Opera House is the glamour queen, with her vast Marc Chagall murals, miles of red carpet, swooshes of stair, and starry chandeliers that swiftly, silently and thrillingly rise to the sky-high gold-leafed ceiling before performances. Avery Fisher Hall caught America's oldest orchestra, the NY Philharmonic, on its trajectory out of Carnegie Hall, while the Juilliard School of Music keeps it supplied with fresh maestri. The New York State Theater, housing the New York City Opera and the New York City Ballet, faces Avery Fisher across the Plaza. Two smaller theatres, the Vivian Beaumont and Mitzi Newhouse, and a more intimate concert hall, Alice Tully, plus the Walter Reade movie theatre, the little Bruno Walter Auditorium and the Guggenheim Bandshell for outdoor summer concerts complete the pack. Over 13,500 arts fans can be swallowed simultaneously. Just don't expect to find a cab after.

HIGHLIGHTS

- Chandeliers in the Met auditorium
- Reflecting Pool with Henry Moore's *Reclining Figure*
- Lincoln Center Out-of-Doors Festival
- NY City Ballet's *Nutcracker*
- Chagall murals, Met foyer
- Thursday morning rehearsals, Avery Fisher
- New York Film Festival
- Philip Johnson's Plaza fountain
- Chamber Music Society, Alice Tully
- Annual *Messiah* sing-along

INFORMATION

- ✚ D3/4
- ✉ Broadway (62nd–67th Streets)
- ☎ 212/875 5400. Met: 212/362 6000. Avery Fisher: 212/875 5030
- ◎ Depends on performance times
- ⑪ Restaurants, cafés, bars
- ⊙ 1, 9 66th Street Lincoln Center
- ▤ M5, M7, M104, crosstown M66
- ♿ Good–excellent. For information: ☎ 212/875 5350
- 💲 Depends on ticket cost; admission to Center free
- ↔ Central Park (▶ 40)
- ❓ Tours leave from concourse under Met, daily 10–5 ☎ 212/875 5350

CENTRAL PARK

INFORMATION

❝*The park's the escape valve on the pressure cooker. Without it New York would explode – especially in summer, when the humidity tops 90 per cent, and bikers, runners, bladers, dog strollers, softball and frisbee players convene. It's a way of life.***❞**

Olmsted, Vaux and the Greensward Plan In the middle of the last century, when there was no Manhattan north of 42nd Street, *New York Evening Post* editor, William Cullen Bryant, campaigned until the city invested the fortune of $5m in an 840-acre wasteland swarming with pig-farming squatters who ran bone-boiling operations. Responsible for clearing the land was journalist Frederick Law Olmsted, who, with English architect Calvert Vaux, also won the competition to design the park, with his 'Greensward Plan'. By day, Olmsted supervised the shifting of 5 million cubic tons of dirt; by night, he and Vaux trod the wasteland acres and designed. Night strolls above 59th Street today are not recommended.

Swings and roundabouts Start at the Dairy Information Center, and pick up a map and events list. These show the lie of the land and tell you about the Wildlife Conservation Center (the Zoo), the Carousel, the playgrounds, rinks, fountains and statues, as well as Strawberry Fields, where John Lennon is commemorated close to the Dakota Building where he lived and was shot. But the busy life of a park rat is not recorded on maps: showing off rollerblade moves on the Mall by the Sheep Meadow; hanging out at the Heckscher Playground and Great Lawn softball leagues; doing the loop road fast, by bike; sunbathing by the vast Lasker Pool in Harlem; playing rowboat dodgems on The Lake; bouldering on the outcrops of Manhattan schist...

FRICK COLLECTION

"Like the Wallace Collection in London and the Musée Picasso in Paris, Henry Clay Frick's mansion is half the reason for seeing his collection. Henry bequeathed these riches to the nation as a memorial to himself – that's the kind of guy he was."

The mansion, and the man Henry Clay Frick was chairman of the Carnegie Steel Corp (US Steel). He was one of the most ruthless strike-breakers of all time and quite the nastiest industrialist of his day. Instead of any come-uppance (though there were several assassination attempts), he got to commission Carrère and Hastings (who designed the NY Public Library) to build him one of the last great *beaux-arts* mansions on Fifth Avenue and fill it with an exquisite collection of 14th- to 19th-century old masters, porcelain, furniture and bronzes. Not much of the furniture is velvet-roped, so you can rest your limbs in a Louis XVI chair before taking a stroll in the central glass-roofed court-yard and gorgeous garden.

What Frick bought Certain rooms of the 40-room mansion are arranged around a particular work or artist, notably the Boucher Room, just east of the entrance, and the Fragonard Room, with the 11-painting *Progress of Love* series. There are British masters (Constable, Whistler, Turner, Gainsborough), Dutch (Vermeer, Rembrandt, Van Eyck, Hals), Italian (Titian, Bellini, Veronese) and Spanish (El Greco, Velázquez, Goya). Interspersed are Limoges enamel and Chinese porcelain, Persian carpets and Marie Antoinette's furniture. Some Frick descendants still have keys to this mod-est *pied à terre*, which, as well as what you see, has a bowling alley in the basement.

HIGHLIGHTS

- *The Progress of Love*, Fragonard
- *Mall in St James's Park*, Gainsborough
- *Sir Thomas More*, Holbein
- *Officer and the Laughing Girl*, Vermeer
- *The Polish Rider*, Rembrandt
- *Virgin and Child with Saints*, Van Eyck
- *Lady Meux*, Whistler
- *Philip IV of Spain*, Velázquez
- The Russell Page garden

INFORMATION

- ⊞ F4
- ✉ 1 E70th Street
- ☎ 212/288 0700
- ◷ Tue–Sat 10–6; Sun 1–6. Closed holidays
- 🍴 None
- Ⓡ 6 68th Street
- 🚌 M1, M2, M3, M4
- ♿ Good
- 🎫 Cheap
- ⟷ Central Park (▶ 40)
- ❓ Lectures: Wed 5:30

Virgin and Child with Saints, Van Eyck

19

WHITNEY MUSEUM OF AMERICAN ART

HIGHLIGHTS

- The Biennial
- *Circus*, Alexander Calder
- The Hoppers
- The O'Keeffes
- *Dempsey and Firpo*, George Bellows
- The Louise Nevelsons
- The drawbridge

INFORMATION

- ✚ F3
- ✉ 945 Madison Avenue
- ☎ 212/570 3600
- ◉ Wed, Fri–Sun 11–6; Thu 1–8. Closed holidays
- 🍴 Café
- 📷 6 77th Street
- 🚌 M1, M2, M3, M4
- ♿ Good
- 💵 Moderate
- ❓ Lectures, video/film. Whitney at the Philip Morris Building ✉ Park Avenue (42nd Street) ☎ 212/878 2550 ◉ Mon–Fri 11–6. Closed holidays

"More modern than the Modern, the Whitney wants to be as unpredictable as the artist du jour, and very often succeeds. It's a New York tradition to sneer at the Biennial, whether or not one has seen the show."

No room at the Met Sculptor and patron of her contemporaries' work, Gertrude Vanderbilt Whitney offered her collection to the Met in 1929, but the great institution turned up its nose and Whitney was forced to found the Whitney. In 1966, Marcel Breuer's cantilevered, granite-clad, Brutalist block was completed to house it in suitably controversial manner, and here it lours still, not universally loved, but impossible to overlook. The Whitney's core collection now reads like a roll-call of the American (and immigrant) greats from earlier this century – Edward Hopper, Thomas Hart Benton, Willem de Kooning, Georgia O'Keeffe, Claes Oldenburg, Jasper Johns, George Bellows and Jackson Pollock are just a few (the male to female ratio has improved, but barely). Let's hope the curators and buyers are as good at spotting talent for the future. There are so many more artists these days…

Lucky dip From the important and delicious collections, work is plucked and hung, oftimes emphasising a single artist's work, while at other times proving more eclectic. There's an active Film and Video department, and two branches (there used to be four branches in Manhattan alone during the art boomtime of the 1980s). The Whitney Biennial (in the spring of odd-numbered years) provides an echo of those days, when the New York art pack gets sweaty debating the merits and demerits of the chosen few on show and of the curator's vision – for the Biennial is invitational, and makes careers.

AMERICAN MUSEUM OF NATURAL HISTORY

❝ *Partly a lovable anachronism, this 125-year-old hulk is stuffed with dinosaur skeletons to pacify bawling brats, but the best things are the blue whale's cocktail bar and the low-tech dioramas. Don't change a thing.* **❞**

Who's who Of the 36 million things owned by the Museum – which is, needless to say, the largest such institution in the world – only a small percentage is on show. Despite its old-fashioned air, the museum is changing, with a $45-million cash injection going mostly into the buildings themselves, cleaning up windows and revealing original features. The Third Floor (where all vertebrate fossils, including dinosaurs, are found), was the first to be renovated, now complete with interactive dinosaurs. There's far too much to see in one day, with three city blocks and the entire evolution of life on earth covered. Not-to-be-missed items include the barosaurus rearing up to her full 55ft to protect her young from a T-rex attack; and, on the first floor, the 94ft blue whale dominates the two-storey Hall of Ocean Life and Biology of Fishes and presides over its own bar.

More gems Another highlight is the 563-carat Star of India blue star sapphire, part of the unbelievable Hall of Meteorites, Minerals and Gems, containing almost $50m worth of precious stones, plus the 34-ton Ahnighito meteorite. The cutest part of the museum, though, is where animals of all sizes are displayed behind glass in *tableaux vivants* (or *tableaux morts*) of considerable artistic merit. Adjoining sub-museums are the astronomy department's Hayden Planetarium, containing the Guggenheim Space Theater and the Sky Theater; and the Nature Max theatre, where a four-storey screen shows ecological blockbusters.

HIGHLIGHTS

- Blue whale
- Barosaurus
- Herd of stuffed elephants
- New dinosaur halls
- Hall of Human Biology and Evolution
- Sky Shows
- Star of India
- The dioramas
- Dinosaur embryo
- The 'Diner Saurus' (fast food)

INFORMATION

- ⊞ E2
- ✉ Central Park West (79th Street)
- ☎ 212/769 5100
- 🕐 Mon–Thu, Sun 10–5:45; Fri–Sat 10–8:45
- 🍴 Three
- Ⓟ B, C 81st Street
- 🚌 M7, M10, M11, M79
- ♿ Good
- 📷 Moderate
- ↔ Lincoln Center (➤ 39), Central Park (➤ 40)
- ❓ 75min tours until 3:15. Hayden Planetarium
  ☎ 212/769 5920

The barosaurus

METROPOLITAN MUSEUM OF ART

HIGHLIGHTS

- Temple of Dendur
- Period rooms, American Wing
- Diptych, Van Eyck
- Young Woman with a Water Jug, Vermeer
- Venus and Adonis, Rubens
- Grand Canal, Venice, Turner
- Sunflowers, Van Gogh
- Madame X, Sargent
- Rooftop Sculpture Garden

The Great Hall

INFORMATION

- ✚ F3
- ✉ 1000 Fifth Avenue (82nd Street)
- ☎ 212/535 7710
- ◷ Tue, Wed, Sun 9:30–5:15; Fri, Sat 9:30–8.45. Closed 25 Dec, 1 Jan
- 🍴 Cafeteria, restaurant, bar
- Ⓢ 4, 5, 6 86th Street
- 🚌 M1, M2, M3, M4
- ♿ Very good
- 💲 Moderate
- ↔ Central Park (➤ 40), Whitney Museum (➤ 42), Guggenheim (➤ 45)
- ❓ The Cloisters (➤ 48) houses more of the Met's medieval collections. Same-day admission on Met ticket

"It'll give you bigger blisters than the Uffizi, bigger chills than the Sistine Chapel, and take a bigger slice of vacation time than all dinners. It's so big, it doesn't just contain Egyptian artefacts, but an entire Egyptian building."

Art city The limestone *beaux-arts* façade with its tremendous steps was a 1902 addition to the Calvert Vaux (of Central Park fame) redbrick Gothic building buried inside here. There are several more building-within-buildings, interior gardens and courtyards, such is the scale of the Met. The 15 BC Temple of Dendur, in its glass-walled bemoated chamber east of the main entrance on the first floor (which Americans view as the second), is the best known, but there's also the Astor Court above it – a replica Ming Dynasty scholar's courtyard. In the American Wing there is a score of period rooms, and the vast and sunlit garden court with its hodgepodge of Tiffany glass and topiary, a Frank Lloyd Wright window and the entire Federal-style façade of the United States Bank from Wall Street.

Where to start? How to stop? A quarter of the 3 million-plus objects are up at any one time, so, pace yourself. Relax. There are about 15 discrete collections. Some visitors decide on one or two per visit – 13th- to 18th-century European Paintings (or part thereof) and Ancient Art, perhaps – and leave it at that. Or you could structure a route around one or two favourite and familiar works. The Information Center in the ground ('first') floor Uris Center, with its Orientation Theater and giant floor plans, is the place to begin, whatever you decide to see. Consider visiting on Friday or Saturday evening, when a string quartet serenades you and the crowds are often thinner.

GUGGENHEIM MUSEUM

"If you could just happen across Frank Lloyd Wright's space-age rotunda, your eyes would pop out of their sockets, but it's the planet's best-known modern building, so you are prepared. Don't forget the museum inside."

Museum of architecture This is the great Frank Lloyd Wright's only New York building, his 'Pantheon', as he called it. It was commissioned by Solomon R Guggenheim at the urging of his longtime friend and taste tutor, Baroness Hilla Rebay von Ehrenwiesen, though the incredibly wealthy metal-mining magnate died ten years before it was completed in 1959. The giant white nautilus is certainly arresting, but it's the interior that unleashes the most superlatives. Take the elevator up, and snake the quarter-mile down the ramp to see why.

Museum of art There are something like 6,000 pieces in the Guggenheim Foundation's possession. Solomon R and his wife Irene Rothschild abandoned the old masters they sought at first, when Hilla Rebay introduced them to Kandinsky, Mondrian and Moholy-Nagy, Léger, Chagall and Gleizes, and they got hooked on the moderns. See also the early Picassos in the small rotunda and the 1992 tower extension, and, if you like the Impressionists and Post-Impressionists, look for the Thannhauser Collection, donated to the museum by art dealer Joseph K Thannhauser and always on display – unlike the Guggenheim holdings, which are rotated.

Branch museum If you want more art, visit the downtown SoHo 'branch' of the Gugg (✉ 575 Broadway ☎ 212/423 3600), which shows one or two temporary exhibitions per year, as well as some more from the collections.

HIGHLIGHTS

- The building
- *L'Hermitage à Pontoise*, Pissarro
- *Paris Through the Window*, Chagall
- *Woman Ironing*, Picasso
- *Nude*, Modigliani
- Kandinskys
- Klees
- Légers
- Downtown Guggenheim
- The shop

INFORMATION

- ✚ G2
- ✉ 1071 Fifth Avenue (88th Street)
- ☎ 212/423 3500
- 🕐 Fri–Wed 10–8. Closed 25 Dec, 1 Jan, Thu
- 🍽 Café
- Ⓜ 4, 5, 6 86th Street
- 🚌 M1, M2, M3, M4
- ♿ Very good
- 💲 Moderate
- ↔ Central Park (➤ 40), Whitney Museum of American Art (➤ 42), Metropolitan Museum of Art (➤ 44)
- ❓ Lecture programme

23

COOPER-HEWITT MUSEUM OF DESIGN

HIGHLIGHTS

- Panelling in the hall
- Solarium
- Garden
- Architectural drawings
- Summer concerts
- Textiles
- Exhibitions

INFORMATION

- ✛ G2
- ✉ 2 E91st Street
- ☎ 212/860 6868
- 🕐 Tue 10–9; Wed–Sat 10–5; Sun noon–5. Closed holidays
- 🍴 None
- Ⓢ 4, 5, 6 86th Street
- 🚌 M1, M2, M3, M4
- ♿ Good
- 💲 Cheap
- ↔ Central Park (➤ 40), Guggenheim Museum (➤ 45)
- ❓ Tours available

Top: the former residence of the industrialist Andrew Carnegie, now home to the Cooper-Hewitt Museum

46

❝*The charming National Museum of Design collections are, Frick-like, housed in an equally charming, wood-panelled mansion. When snow falls in the holiday season, there's nowhere better to indulge in mawkishly nostalgic reveries.***❞**

Carnegie-Hewitt The mansion belonged to industrialist Andrew Carnegie, who, in 1903, had asked architects Babb, Cook & Willard for 'the most modest, plainest, and most roomy house in New York City'. This he did not receive (apart from the roominess), since this little château was built with mod cons galore – central heating, air-conditioning and elevators – and a big-gated garden to keep out the squatter neighbours. The entire neighbourhood came to be known as Carnegie Hill, thanks to his early patronage. Andrew's wife, Louise, lived here till her death in 1946, then, some 20 years later, the Carnegie Corporation donated it to the Smithsonian Institution to house the Hewitt sisters' collections. Still following? The three sisters, Amy, Eleanor and Sarah, had become infatuated with the V&A on a visit to London in 1897, which set them off on their lifelong collecting spree.

And Cooper The girls' grandpa was Peter Cooper, founder of the Cooper Union college of art and architecture, and he offered the collection a home there, where it stayed until 1967. The contemporary Cooper-Hewitt is a vibrant institution where all manner of events are laid on. In addition to the collections, some of which are on display (though it's hard to predict which), there are various reference resources, including the country's biggest architectural drawings collection, a textile library with a 3,000-year span, auction catalogues, wallpapers, jewellery, earthenware – you name it.

YANKEE STADIUM

"*Final out, bottom of the Ninth and, whether the home team has won or lost, Sinatra's 'New York, New York' wafts over the blue seats. Baseball embodies the American spirit: this stadium is New York.***"**

What baseball means New Yorkers are sports mad, even though a team nowadays is almost as much a brand name as a unit of athletes. Professional baseball today is a big-bucks business, which reached its apogee of heartlessness with the players strike of 1994. To Yankee fans – already licking wounds inflicted by unpopular team owner, George Steinbrenner – this signalled the end of baseball, and thus of America. Their 1996 world series victory, however, made the world turn again.

The house that Ruth built If you want to see what makes the New York heart tick (unless it belongs to a fan of the 1962 upstart National League NY Mets), go and see a Yankees home game. The Yankees dominated the early eras of baseball. In 1920, George Herman 'Babe' Ruth joined the team and quickly became a hero of such mythic stature that his popularity built them a stadium in 1923 (renovated in the mid-1970s).

Where have you gone, Joe Di Maggio? The Babe's No 3 is only one of the 'retired' numbers that honour great players who bore them and that will never be re-allocated. Lou Gehrig was No 4 (killed by the disease they named after him); No 5 was Joe Di Maggio's (he married Marilyn Monroe and pulled off a 56-game hitting streak); No 7 was Mickey Mantle's, and No 8 was Yogi Berra's. These four played between 1946 and 1960, when the team won eight World Series titles; they are why Yankee fans 'bleed pinstripes'.

HIGHLIGHTS

- Don Mattingly, former first baseman
- The Bleachers (cheap seats)
- Seventh Inning Stretch (mid-game break for spectators)
- Eddie Layton, organist
- 'Giveaway Days'

INFORMATION

- ✚ Off map at H1
- ✉ E 161st Street, Bronx
- ☎ 718/293 4300. Ticketmaster: 212/307 1212
- ◷ Season runs Apr–Oct. Check schedule for home games
- 🍴 Concession stands
- Ⓢ 4, D, C (weekdays) 161st Street
- 🚌 BX6, BX13, BX55
- ♿ Good
- 💰 Expensive

47

THE CLOISTERS

HIGHLIGHTS

- Unicorn Tapestries
- Fuentidueña Chapel
- Cuxa Cloister
- Saint Guilhem Cloister
- Annunciation Altarpiece
- Boppard stained glass
- Rosary bead carved with the Passion
- Bonnefont Cloister herb garden
- Ramparts – views to Hudson

INFORMATION

- ✚ Off map at F1
- ✉ Fort Tryon Park, North Manhattan
- ☎ 718/923 3700
- 🕐 Nov–Feb Tue–Sun 9:30–4.45. Mar–Oct Tue–Sun 9:30-5:15. Closed holidays
- 🚇 A 190th Street
- 🚌 M4
- ♿ Good
- 💲 Moderate
- ❓ Tours: Tue–Fri 3; Sun noon. Joint same-day admission with the Met. The Cloisters offers a concert programme of live and recorded medieval music

"A 12th-century Spanish apse, attached to a Romanesque cloister and a Gothic chapel – what's all this doing in the Bronx? This is the Met's medieval branch: the incongruity is hallucinogenic, and amazing enough in itself, but the sights are just heavenly."

Medieval world The building in Fort Tryon Park – a site in the far north of Manhattan Island that was donated by Rockefeller Jr – is not medieval, you'll be astonished to learn, but there are plenty of parts of buildings inside it that are. The 12th-century pink-stone Cuxa Cloister was liberated from the French Pyrenees, and the 3,000 limestone blocks of the Fuentidueña Chapel apse were rescued from the ruins of the church of Saint-Martín in Spain. The Cloisters are not some Disney-esque simulacrum of medieval Europe, however. Being able to gaze at the ribbed vaulting of the late-Romanesque Pontaut Chapter House, or strolling past the early Flemish Annunciation Altarpiece of Robert Campin to the familiar 15th-century Unicorn Tapestries are treats that have not been possible in Europe since the Age of Chivalry exhibition at London's Royal Academy gathered together high points of medieval art some years ago.

Through the ages The collections are arranged chronologically, so that one can trace not only the metamorphosis of architectural styles, but also of the medieval mind – by turns awestruck, playful, bawdy and terrified. The bulk of the art and architecture was amassed by sculptor George Gray Bernard early this century. Much was rescued from ruin – the effigy of the Crusader, Jean d'Alluye, for instance, was doing duty as a bridge, while the priceless Unicorn Tapestries were once draped over fruit trees as frost blankets.

NEW YORK's *best*

BUILDINGS

Reach for the sky

The tallest building in the world is the Sears Roebuck Tower in Chicago, but in their day the following New York structures were the highest: Park Row Building (✉ 15 Park Row, 1899–1908, 386ft), Chrysler Building (➤ 35, 1929–30, 1,048ft), Empire State Building (➤ 33, 1930–72, 1,250ft), World Trade Center Towers (➤ 28, 1972–79, 1,350ft). Contrary to popular myth, the Flatiron was never the tallest.

The Lower Manhattan skyline, dominated by the twin towers of the World Trade Center

CATHEDRAL OF ST JOHN THE DIVINE
Started in 1892, and not finished yet, this would be the world's biggest.
✚ Off map at G1 ✉ Amsterdam Avenue, W112th Street ☎ 212/316 7540 🕐 Mon–Sat 7AM–5PM; Sun 7AM–8PM 🚇 1, 9 110th Street

CITICORP CENTER
The 45-degree lightbox is one of the skyline's greatest hits at night. The four-legged base shelters St Peter's Church and the great atrium.
✚ F6 ✉ 153 E53rd Street 🚇 6 51st Street

THE DAKOTA
First of the great Upper West Side luxury apartment blocks, designed by Henry Hardenberg, but famous as John Lennon's murder site.
✚ E3 ✉ 1 W72nd Street (Central Park West) 🚇 B, C 72nd Street

FLATIRON BUILDING

A 1902 skyscraper named after its amazing shape: an isosceles triangle with a sharp angle pointing uptown.

🟦 D8 ✉ 175 Fifth Avenue (E22nd/23rd Streets) Ⓜ N, R 23rd Street

LEVER HOUSE

The Seagram and this 1952 Skidmore, Owings & Merrill building were precursors of all glass blocks.

🟦 E5 ✉ 390 Park Avenue (53rd/54th Streets) ☎ 212/960 4685
🕐 Lobby: Mon–Fri 10–5; Sun 1–5 Ⓜ E, F Fifth Avenue

'LIPSTICK BUILDING'

This likeable 1986 show-off is by John Burgee with Philip Johnson.

🟦 F5 ✉ 885 Third Avenue (55/56th Streets) Ⓜ 6 51st Street

METLIFE BUILDING

Known to New Yorkers as the Pan Am Building – which it was until 1981. It's by Bauhaus priest Walter Gropius, plus Emery Roth & Sons and Pietro Belluschi.

🟦 E6 ✉ 200 Park Avenue (44/45th Streets) Ⓜ 4, 5, 6, 7 42nd Street

NY STOCK EXCHANGE

The neo-classical façade dates only from 1903. See trading from the gallery and recall the Crash of 1929.

🟦 A13 ✉ 20 Broad Street ☎ 212/656 5167 🕐 Mon–Fri 9:15–4
Ⓜ 2, 3, 4, 5 Wall Street; 1, 9 Rector Street; J, M, Z Broad Street
🎟 Free

SEAGRAM BUILDING

Mies van der Rohe's 1958 bronze glazed tower is *the* Modernist landmark. Philip Johnson interiors.

🟦 E5/6 ✉ 375 Park Avenue (52nd/53rd Streets) ☎ 212/572 7000 🕐 Tour: Tue 3PM 🍴 Two Ⓜ E, F Fifth Avenue 🎟 Free

TRUMP TOWER

'Glitzy' captured in pink marble and glass.

🟦 E5 ✉ 725 Fifth Avenue (56th Street) ☎ 212/832 2000
🕐 8AM–10PM 🍴 Several Ⓜ E, F Fifth Avenue 🎟 Free

UNITED NATIONS HEADQUARTERS

Officially outside the USA, this vast 1947–63 complex included Le Corbusier among its architects.

🟦 F6/7 ✉ First Avenue (45th Street) ☎ 212/963 7713
🕐 Fri–Wed 9:15–4:45. Closed weekends Jan–Feb, 1 Jan, 25 Dec
🍴 Café, restaurant Ⓜ 4, 5, 6, 7 42nd Street, Grand Central 🎟 Free

WORLD FINANCIAL CENTER

Cesar Pelli's waterfront World Trade Center neighbour includes the fab Winter Garden atrium.

🟦 A12 ✉ 200 Liberty Street ☎ 212/945 0505 🍴 Many Ⓜ 1, 9, N, R Cortlandt Street; A, C, E Chambers Street; 4, 5 Fulton Street
🎟 Free

The Flatiron Building was one of the first structures to be erected around a steel frame – the basic support of every subsequent skyscraper

51

OF THE OLD

See Top 25 Sights for
FRICK MANSION ▶ 41
SCHERMERHORN ROW,
      SOUTH STREET SEAPORT ▶ 27

St Patrick's Cathedral

BLOCK BEAUTIFUL

This picturesque, tree-lined 1920s row really is called this. Also see the pretty square near by, centred on private Gramercy Park (▶ 54). ⊞ D8 ✉ E19th Street (Irving Place/Third Avenue) 🚇 N, R 14th Street Union Square; 6 23rd Street

CITY HALL

French Renaissance-style façade and an elegant Georgian interior – see it by visiting the Governor's room, with small furniture museum. ⊞ B12 ✉ Broadway (Murray Street) ☎ 212/788 3000 🕐 Mon–Fri 10–3:30 🚇 2, 3 Park Place; 4, 5, 6 Brooklyn Bridge/City Hall; N, R City Hall 🆓 Free

ST PATRICK'S CATHEDRAL

James Renwick's Gothic Revival cathedral is the US's biggest for Catholics. ⊞ E5/6 ✉ Fifth Avenue (50th Street) ☎ 212/753 2261 🕐 6AM–9PM 🚇 6 51st Street; E, F Fifth Ave 🆓 Free

SINGER BUILDING & HAUGHWOUT STORE

Two of the best ambassadors for the SoHo Cast Iron Historic District (▶ 54) – the 26 blocks of skyscraper forerunners, now galleries and posh boutiques. The Haughwout had the first Otis steam elevator. ⊞ C10 ✉ Singer: 561 Broadway. Haughwout: 488 Broadway 🚇 N, R Prince Street; B, D, F, Q Broadway/Lafayette

WASHINGTON SQUARE: 'THE ROW' AND ARCH

'The Row' (1–13, North side) housed movers and shakers of early 19th-century New York city – read Henry James's *Washington Square* for details. ⊞ C9 ✉ South end of Fifth Avenue 🚇 N, R 8th Street; A, C, E, B, D, F, Q W4th Street

WOOLWORTH BUILDING

The world's tallest until the Chrysler, Cass Gilbert's Gothic beauty has NYC's richest lobby – see witty bas reliefs of both architect and tycoon. ⊞ B12 ✉ 233 Broadway 🕐 Lobby: Mon–Fri 7–6. Closed holidays 🚇 2, 3 Park Place; N, R City Hall

Literary New York

Old New York is the title of a collection of Edith Wharton novellas that brings to life the *Age of Innocence* (the Wharton novel filmed by Scorsese). The other chronicler of 19th-century New York manners was, of course, Henry James, especially in *Washington Square* (filmed as *The Heiress*). For the jazz age of the 1920s, read F Scott Fitzgerald's short stories.

VIEWS

BROOKLYN HEIGHTS ESPLANADE

As traffic clogs the Brooklyn–Queens Expressway beneath your feet, all is serene on this elegantissimo promenade, with some of New York's most covetable houses and very rare gardens at your back and Manhattan's financial centre spread out before you.

➕ Off map at C14 ✉ West end of Clark Street 🚇 2, 3 Clark Street

PARK AVENUE FROM CARNEGIE HILL

The view from here to the MetLife building is best experienced during the Christmas holiday season when pine trees bedecked with sparkling white lights bisect the route.

➕ G2 🚇 6 86th Street (96th Street)

ROOSEVELT ISLAND TRAMWAY

One of New York City's oddities is this Swiss-made cable car, which has been flying passengers to the site of the NYC Lunatic Asylum (undergoing restoration) and on into Queens since 1976.

➕ F5 ✉ Second Avenue (60th Street) ☎ 212/832 4543
🕐 Mon–Fri 6AM–2AM; weekends 6AM–3AM 🚇 B, Q Lexington Avenue
💲 Inexpensive

STATEN ISLAND FERRY

Those three words 'Staten Island Ferry' are nearly always followed by these three: 'city's best bargain'. The voyage is a tiny vacation.

➕ A14 ✉ Whitehall Terminal
☎ 212/806 6901, 718/390 5253 🕐 24hr service 🚇 N, R Whitehall Street South Ferry
💲 Inexpensive

WORLD FINANCIAL CENTER (► 51)

Join the Wall Street hordes in the piazza for sunset over the Hudson.

A table with a view

This is a sought-after commodity. Eat well too (and pay handsome sums) at Brooklyn's River Café (✉ 1 Water Street ☎ 718/522 5200) or the Water's Edge in Queens (✉ 44th Drive, East River, Long Island City ☎ 718/482 0033), with its free boat taxi and floor-to-ceiling windows. The Water Club (✉ 500 E30th Street ☎ 212/683 3333) has a view in the other direction, and new American food. Or dine waterside on a more modest budget at the Boathouse Café (☎ 212/517 2233) on Central Park's lake.

Lower Manhattan and the East River viewed from Brooklyn Heights

NEIGHBOURHOODS

TriBeCa

The East Village

Not so much a neighbourhood as a state of mind – the one that parents hope is just a phase. At the time of writing, pierced lips, nipples, navels and other body parts were *de rigueur*, and tattoos were old hat. The streets themselves are bursting with cheap and good restaurants, sleazy bars, coffee lounges, vintage clothing stores and wholefood emporia. Pretty Tompkins Square Park has great concerts in summer.

See Top 25 Sights for
CHINATOWN ► 30
GREENWICH VILLAGE ► 31

EAST VILLAGE
Somewhat tamer than it used to be, but if you're over 30 and not in black, you still feel odd.
➕ D/E10 🚇 F 2nd Avenue; 6 Astor Place

GRAMERCY PARK AND FLATIRON
The former – peaceful and pleasant to stroll – is centred on the eponymous park; the latter on the eponymous building (► 51). It's grown out of the photography district, hangout of models, and the new Restaurant Row is Park Avenue South.
➕ D8 🚇 N, R, 6 23rd Street

LITTLE ITALY
Reduced to Mulberry Street, this is a nice place to stroll and café-hop. Skip the touristy red-sauce spaghetterias, and see Scorsese's *Mean Streets* for the real thing. Adjacent streets have become the latest trendy area, especially Elizabeth Street between Prince and Houston Streets.
➕ C10/11 🚇 6 Spring Street

LOWER EAST SIDE
Where the melting pot landed; the birth of Jewish New York is Orchard Street.
➕ D/E11/12 🚇 F Delancey Street

SOHO
South of Houston (say '*How*-stun') saw 1980s art mania, when its gorgeous cast-iron-framed buildings were 'loft-ised' on the cheap. Now it's all expensive boutique shopping, gallery-hopping, and posing.
➕ B/C10 🚇 N, R Prince Street; C, E Spring Street

THEATER/GARMENT DISTRICT
As it sounds. It is delineated more or less by Sixth and Ninth avenues and 34th to 59th Streets, with theatres clustering on – where else? – Broadway, and the 'garmentos' – those who work in the fashion trade – along Seventh Avenue.
➕ D5/6 and C/D6 🚇 N, R, 1, 2, 3 Times Square

TRIBECA
Like SoHo, the Flatiron and the East Village, the 'Triangle Below Canal' was designated a neighbourhood by real estate agents, but the sobriquet stuck. Once a windy wasteland of warehouses, now it has the top tables (Bouley, Nobu, Chanterelle), plus rich architects, artists and filmmakers in lofts.
➕ A/B10 🚇 A, 1, 2, 3 Chambers Street

MUSEUMS

FORBES MAGAZINE GALLERIES
Toy soldiers and Fabergé eggs, plus art.
➕ C9 ✉ 63 Fifth Avenue (12th Street) ☎ 212/206 5548 🕐 Tue, Wed, Fri, Sat 10–4 🚇 4, 5, 6 14th Street 💷 Free

JEWISH MUSEUM
Chronicling Jewish experience worldwide, with artefacts dating back 4,000 years.
➕ G2 ✉ 1109 Fifth Avenue ☎ 212/423 3200 🕐 Sun–Thu 11–5:45, Tue till 8PM 🍴 Café 🚇 4, 5, 6 86th Street 💷 Moderate

LOWER EAST SIDE TENEMENT MUSEUM
A reconstruction of life in this 1863 tenement block, plus talks, tours, etc.
➕ D11 ✉ 97 Orchard Street ☎ 212/431 0233
🕐 Tue–Fri 11–4, Sun 10–5 🚇 F, J, M, Z Delancey Street; B, D, Q Grand Street 💷 Inexpensive

NEW MUSEUM OF CONTEMPORARY ART
What MoMA stops at, Whitney shows; where Whitney balks, this starts.
➕ C10 ✉ 583 Broadway (Houston/Prince Streets)
☎ 212/219 1222 🕐 Wed–Sun noon–6; Sat noon–8 🚇 N, R Prince Street 💷 Cheap

NEW YORK CITY FIRE MUSEUM
See the firefighting dog! Pretty *beaux-arts* station.
➕ B10 ✉ 278 Spring Street, SoHo ☎ 212/691 1303 🕐 Tue–Sat 10–4 🚇 C, E Spring Street 💷 Contribution

PIERPONT MORGAN LIBRARY
McKim, Mead & White's 1902 palazzo for Morgan's sublime manuscripts.
➕ D/E7 ✉ 29 E36th Street ☎ 212/685 0008 🕐 Tue–Sat 10:30–5; Sun 1–5 🚇 6 33rd Street 💷 Moderate

POLICE ACADEMY MUSEUM
See Al Capone's gun and learn about Prohibition raids – maybe from a cop.
➕ D8 ✉ 235 E20th Street ☎ 212/477 9753 🕐 Mon–Fri 9–3. Call first 🚇 4, 5, 6 14th Street 💷 Free

Musical soirées
This innovation is catching on quickly at major museums. The Metropolitan Museum of Art started the whole thing, and among those to have jumped on the bandwagon are: the Guggenheim (uptown), with jazz in Frank Lloyd Wright's rotunda; the Metropolitan's Cloisters outpost; and the Frick, with chamber music in its beautiful courtyard.

New York City Fire Museum

GALLERIES & OUTDOOR ART

Red Cube, *by Isamu Noguchi, Church Street*

Outside art

Save time: combine art with sightseeing.

Stabile (1971), Alexander Calder (📍 A12 ✉ 6 World Trade Center)

Group of Four Trees (1972), Jean Dubuffet (📍 B12 ✉ Chase Manhattan Bank, Pine/Nassau/ Liberty Streets)

Gay Liberation (1980), George Segal (📍 B9 ✉ Christopher Park, Sheridan Square)

Prometheus (1934), Paul Manship (📍 E5 ✉ Rockefeller Center)

Single Form (1964), Barbara Hepworth (📍 F7 ✉ Pool of Secretariat Building, UN, First Avenue at 46th Street)

Reclining Figure (1965), Henry Moore (📍 D4 ✉ Reflecting Pool, Lincoln Center)

Night Presence IV (1972), Louise Nevelson (📍 G2 ✉ Park Avenue at 92nd Street)

SOHO GALLERIES

Doing the SoHo galleries, brunch and shopping (in a different order of importance) is one version of the quintessential New York Saturday. A few galleries have moved to West Chelsea, or uptown. The following are still here, and are major. (Call for current show.)

🕐 Generally Tue–Sat 11–6 🚇 N, R Prince Street; C, E Spring Street

Dia Center for the Arts	✉ 393 W Broadway	☎ 212/925 9397
Gagosian	✉ 136 Wooster Street	☎ 212/228 2878
Leo Castelli	✉ 420 W Broadway	☎ 212/431 5160
Leo Castelli II	✉ 578 Broadway	☎ 212/431 6279
Meisel	✉ 141 Prince Street	☎ 212/677 1340
Sonnabend	✉ 420 W Broadway	☎ 212/966 6160
Vorpal	✉ 459 W Broadway	☎ 212/334 3939
Ward-Nasse	✉ 178 Prince Street	☎ 212/925 6951

CHELSEA GALLERIES

The newest art district is way west.

Marks	✉ 522 W22nd Street	☎ 212/243 0200
Paula Cooper	✉ 534 W21st Street	☎ 212/255 1105
Team	✉ 527 W26th Street	☎ 212/279 9219

UPTOWN GALLERIES

Dressier than Chelsea or SoHo viewing.

Fischbach	✉ 24 W57th Street	☎ 212/759 2345
Gagosian	✉ 980 Madison Avenue	☎ 212/744 2313
Janis	✉ 110 W57th Street	☎ 212/586 0110
Marlborough	✉ 40 W57th Street	☎ 212/541 4900
Mary Boone	✉ 745 5th Avenue	☎ 212/752 2929
Pace	✉ 32 E57th Street	☎ 212/421 3292

FOR KIDS

BRONX ZOO

The biggest city zoo in the US has 4,000 animals, a kid's zoo and a monorail.

➕ Off map at I1 ✉ Fordham Road (Bronx River Parkway Northeast) ☎ 718/367 1010 🕐 Apr–Oct 10–5. Nov–Mar 10–4:30 🍴 Restaurant 🚇 2, 5 Pelham Parkway 💷 Moderate

CHILDREN'S MUSEUM OF THE ARTS

Highlights: the Monet Ballpond, Architects Alley and the Wonder Theater.

➕ C11 ✉ 72 Spring Street ☎ 212/274 0986 🕐 Tue–Sun 11–5 🚇 6 Spring Street 💷 Moderate

CHILDREN'S MUSEUM OF MANHATTAN

Ignore the word 'museum' – here they can make their own TV show.

➕ D5 ✉ 212 W83rd Street ☎ 212/721 1234 🕐 Sep–May Mon, Wed, Thu 1:30–5:30; Fri–Sun 10–5. Jun–Aug Wed–Mon 10–5 🚇 4, 5, 6 86th Street 💷 Moderate

FAO SCHWARZ

The world's most famous toyshop – see the movie *Big*; set advance spending and time limits. The giant singing clock at the entrance is scary.

➕ E5 ✉ 767 Fifth Avenue ☎ 212/644 9400 🕐 Mon–Sat 9–9; Sun 10–8 🚇 E, F Fifth Avenue; 4, 6 59th Street 💷 Free

HARLEY DAVIDSON CAFÉ AND PLANET HOLLYWOOD

Two shameless pack-em-in theme canteens that ten-year-olds adore. Also check out the supermodel-owned Fashion Café in Rockefeller Centre.

➕ E5 ✉ 1370 Sixth Avenue (W56th Street) ☎ 212/245 6000 ✉ 140 W57th Street ☎ 212//333–7827 🕐 Daily till late 🚇 N, R, B, Q 57th Street 💷 Moderate

SERENDIPITY 3 (➤ 68)

WONDERCAMP

This vast multi-activity centre is the perfect place to leave the children while you hit the Met.

➕ D8 ✉ 27 W23rd Street ☎ 212/243 1111 🕐 Sun–Thu 10–6:30; Fri, Sat 10–9 🚇 N, R, F 23rd Street 💷 Moderate

Kids' Broadway

All over town are theatrical troupes dedicated to the entertainment of youth. Try:

The Paper Bag Players

☎ 212/362 0431. Winter season at Symphony Space:

✉ Broadway (95th Street)

☎ 212/864 6400

New York Children's Theater

✉ 250 W65th Street

☎ 212/496 8009

Theaterworks/USA

✉ Broadway (76th Street)

☎ 212/677 5959

Little People's Theater

✉ 39 Grove Street

☎ 212/765 9540

FREE THINGS

On Parade

New York loves a parade, and nobody does it more often than New Yorkers. The biggest are:

St Patrick's Day Parade (✉ Fifth Avenue, 44th–86th Streets 🕐 17 Mar);

Easter Parade (✉ Fifth Avenue, 44th–59th Streets 🕐 Easter Sun);

Lesbian & Gay Pride Day Parade (✉ Fifth Avenue,

Street entertainment: a sound return for a small investment

Columbus Circle–Washington Square 🕐 late Jun);

Columbus Day Parade (✉ Fifth Avenue, 44–86th Streets 🕐 12 Oct);

Hallowe'en Parade (✉ Greenwich Village 🕐 31 Oct);

Macy's Thanksgiving Day Parade (Central Park West, 79th Street–Broadway, 34th Street 🕐 Fourth Thu in Nov).

See Top 25 Sights for
CENTRAL PARK ➤ 40
COOPER-HEWITT (TUE EVENING FREE) ➤ 46
FULTON FISH MARKET, SOUTH STREET SEAPORT ➤ 27
GUGGENHEIM MUSEUM (THU 6–8PM PAY-WHAT-YOU-WISH) ➤ 45
MUSEUM OF MODERN ART (THU 5–9PM PAY-WHAT-YOU-WISH) ➤ 38
NEW YORK PUBLIC LIBRARY ➤ 34

BEING ON TV
Write in advance for free tickets to talk shows, etc.
✉ NBC, 30 Rockefeller Plaza ☎ 212/664 3056 🚇 B, D, F 47th–50th Streets

BIG APPLE GREETERS
Volunteers who like showing off their city will take you to places in NYC for free.
☎ 212/669 3602 or 212/669 8273. 48 hours' notice required

BROOKLYN BOTANIC GARDEN
A 52-acre expanse with herbs, roses, fragrant flora especially for the blind, and Shakespeare, kids' and Japanese gardens.
✚ Off map at F14 ✉ 1000 Washington Avenue ☎ 718/622 4433 🕐 Apr–Sep Tue–Fri 8–6; weekends 10–6. Oct–Mar Tue–Fri 8–4:30; weekends 10–4:30 🍴 Café 🚇 2, 3 Eastern Parkway

BRYANT PARK
The summer evening 'walk-in' movies are a new tradition; also concerts.
✚ D6 🚇 B, D, F, 42nd Street

FORBES MAGAZINE GALLERIES (➤ 55)

NY STOCK EXCHANGE GALLERY (➤ 51)

SOHO GALLERY HOPPING (➤ 56)

STATEN ISLAND FERRY (➤ 53)
The 50¢ round-trip counts as free!

WALKING
The world's best walking city. You'll need around two minutes per block, comfortable shoes and sunglasses.

WASHINGTON SQUARE (➤ 52)
In summer it's live theatre – literally. Genuinely funny stand-ups perform.

WORLD FINANCIAL CENTER (➤ 51)
The Winter Garden Atrium has events all year round.

GYMS

CHELSEA PIERS SPORTS CENTRE
Egalitarian, vast, packed with a four-tier golf range, two ice-skating rinks, marina, climbing wall, track and field arena, big swimming pool.
➕ B7 ✉ Piers 59–62 West Side Highway 🚇 C, E, 23rd Street

CRUNCH
Cyberpunk styling, gimmicks (live DJs, haircutting, heart-rate monitors), downtown attitude. Best classes: Terry Southerland's Knockout Boxing, Thighs and Gossip, Spinning – massed stationary bike riding.
➕ D9 ✉ 54 E13th Street (and other branches) ☎ 212/475 2018 🚇 N, R, 4, 6 Union Square

EQUINOX
Everyone's good-looking, and a fair bit of eyeing goes on – but what the heck, those bodies took *work*. Best classes: Patricia Moreno's; Michael Olajidé Jr's Aerobox. Uptown's spa has cranio-sacral massage, acupuncture, Rolfing...
➕ D3 ✉ 897 Broadway (and other branches) ☎ 212/780 9300 🚇 N, R 23rd Street

PRINTING HOUSE
A friendly sort of place with classes, a rooftop pool, squash courts and sundeck.
➕ B9 ✉ 421 Hudson Street ☎ 212/243 7600 🚇 1, 2, 3, 9 Houston Street

REEBOK SPORTS CLUB NY
Everything from ski and windsurfing simulators to a fancy bistro, and huge prices.
➕ D4 ✉ Near Lincoln Center 🚇 1, 2, 3, 9 66th Street

VANDERBILT YMCA
Classes, two good pools and no snooty attitude.
➕ F6 ✉ 224 E47th Street ☎ 212/756 9600 🚇 6 51st Street

WORLD
Half spiritual haven, half professional iron-pumper's heaven, it's light and spacious, and it's open 24 hours. Best classes: You & Me Yoga (doubles isn't just tennis), NIA (Neuro-Muscular Integrative Action – don't ask), Breathe!
➕ D3 ✉ 1926 Broadway (plus branch) ☎ 212/874 0942 🚇 1, 2, 3, 9 66th Street

Where do you work out?

Many of the things people did during the 1980s at frenetic all-night dance clubs – meet, sweat, schmooze, pose – are now accomplished at the gym. All New Yorkers have gym membership and most use it. 'Where do you work out?' is a perfectly reasonable question, as unsurprising as the sight of people bouncing rhythmically in upstairs windows.

The New York gym provides more than just exercise: it's a way of life

59

'ONLY IN NEW YORK'

BARNEY'S WAREHOUSE SALE

Warehouse sales are known elsewhere, but you must understand, Barney's is *the* store where every single New Yorker bar none aspires to shop for clothes. Consequently, *everyone* goes to this event. It's a zoo.

✚ C8 ✉ 255 W17th Street ◷ Feb, Sep ⊕ 1,9 18th Street

BASKETBALL STARS ON THE STREET

At 'The Cage', you can see basketball played by *future* stars, as good as the pros (and it's free).

✚ B10 ✉ Sixth Avenue (W3rd Street) ⊕ A, B, C, D, E, F W4th Street

GRAND MARCH OF THE DACHSHUNDS

This is the climax of the two-hour Dachshund Octoberfest (usually noon on the third Saturday). The dogs parade around the fountain.

✚ C9 ✉ Washington Square Park ⊕ N, R 8th Street

HOWARD STERN

If he didn't invent the genre of 'shock jock', this irritating, self-consciously controversial individual certainly popularised it. To hear him, tune into 92.3FM WXRK weekday mornings.

Macy's Thanksgiving Day Parade

MACY'S THANKSGIVING DAY PARADE BALLOON INFLATION

Macy's Thanksgiving Day Parade (fourth Thursday in November) is fine, but better are the impromptu street parties that convene the night before, as the balloons go up.

✚ E2 ✉ Central Park West around 81st Street ⊕ C 81st Street

POETRY SLAMS

These are competitive poetry readings. One night a week (Friday is normal), writers declaim, chant and even sing their work to raucous crowds.

✚ D10 ✉ Nuyorican Poets Café, 236 E3rd Street (Avenues B/C) ☎ 212/505 8183 ⊕ F Second Avenue

RUSSIAN BATHS

This has been here for ever, and looks that way in the Stone Room (hot as hell) where you get your schwitze – a beating with soapy oak leaves.

✚ D10 ✉ 268 E10th Street ☎ 212/473 8806 ⊕ 6 Astor Place

Wigstock

This fab Labor Day fest is as it sounds – an excuse to wear wild wigs and wild drag. RuPaul started here. Started in 1984, it has now outgrown its venue.

NEW YORK
where to...

NEW YORK SWANK

Prices

The restaurants on the following pages are in three price categories:

£££   over $50 per person

££ $30–50 per person

£   up to $30 per person

Spoilt for choice?

In a city with 17,000 restaurants, there's no need to share anyone else's preferences, even if they inhabit the same block. All New Yorkers are restaurant experts, because all New Yorkers eat out more often than in (and eating in usually means ordering in). They throw dinner parties at restaurants, they eat alone with a book at the best tables, and their repertoire includes options for both. Listings can never do justice to the depth of choice in this town.

FOUR SEASONS (£££)

Take advantage of the 'Grill at Night' deal, where the notable Philip Johnson interior (this is in the Seagram Building) becomes an affordable sight. However, the Pool Room is a finer sight, and is the place to be at night, so you can't win unless you pay up. Food is state-of-the-art American-trendy, using things like *mahi-mahi* (meaty white fish), *verjus* (a vine by-product), and named chillies, but all in the appropriate season.

✚ E6 ✉ 99 E52nd Street (Park/Lexington Avenues) ☎ 212/754 9494 🕐 Closed Sun, Sat lunch 🚇 6 51st Street

LE CIRQUE 2000 (£££)

The venerable Le Cirque moved and had not reopened at the time of writing, but certain things never change. You come not to have a private experience, but to be fêted by waiters, dazzled by yourselves and to ogle other tables of maybe models, power brokers or Hollywooders. Owner, Sirio Maccioni, wields more glamour than his chef, Sylvain Portay – the *foie gras* style, finished with compulsory crème brûlée.

✚ F4 ✉ New York Palace Hotel, 455 Madison Avenue (51st Street) ☎ 212/794 9292 🕐 Closed Sun 🚇 51st Street

LES CÉLÉBRITÉS (£££)

So pretty it's like eating inside a Fabergé egg from the Forbes Galleries, except that this egg's hung with art by célébrités like James Dean. But Christian Delouvrier's beautifully presented, exquisite cuisine is the biggest celebrity – spun sugar shapes, seafood shells, sauce paintings, etc.

✚ E5 ✉ Essex House Hotel, 155 W58th Street (Sixth/Seventh Avenues) ☎ 212/ 484 5113 🕐 Tue–Sat, dinner 🚇 N, R 57th Street

LESPINASSE (£££)

Gray Kunz's French food lightened by Asian sensibility is exquisite and exclusive, and served like plate art. Everything here is luxurious from the armchair comfort to the pampering service.

✚ E5 ✉ St Regis Hotel, 2 E55th Street (Fifth/Madison Avenues) ☎ 212/339 6719 🕐 Daily 🚇 6 51st Street

LUTÈCE (£££)

Even after 30-plus years, even after being sold to a restaurant group, Lutèce still offers classic French cooking at its best. Saddle of rabbit with wild mushrooms, tarte tatin – satisfying and unpretentious, like the atmosphere.

✚ F6 ✉ 249 E50th Street (Second/Third Avenues) ☎ 212/752 2225 🕐 Closed Mon, Sat lunch, Sun 🚇 6 51st Street

RIVER CAFÉ (£££)

Tear your eyes from the Lower Manhattan skyline view and you'll find an original mind has been tinkering with American ingredients on your plate, leading to, say, fruitwood-smoked salmon on a johnnycake, or something with buffalo, wild mushrooms, fresh berries...

✚ C13 ✉ 1 Water Street (East River) ☎ 718/522 5200 🕐 Daily 🚇 A High Street

FOODIE SHRINES

DANIEL (£££)

Daniel Boulud is young, driven and French, and his cool and calm Upper East Side salon appeals greatly to gourmet grown-ups. His style is simultaneously cutting-edge and serious, littered with luxe ingredients: oyster velouté with sea urchins and caviar; a risotto of lobster, courgette flowers and artichokes; truffled sweetbreads…

🔲 F3 ✉ E. 76th Street (Fifth/Madison Avenues) ☎ 212/288–0033 🕐 Closed Sun 🚇 77th Street

GOTHAM BAR AND GRILL (££–£££)

This soaring space on the edge of Greenwich Village is appropriately named, since Alfred Portale has won the 'build the tallest food' competition. Of course, his creations soar not only architecturally. They also taste fine: red snapper balances on Manila clams, rack of lamb on garlic mash. This is Gotham City cuisine in a place to be seen.

🔲 C9 ✉ 12 E12th Street (Fifth Avenue) ☎ 212/620 4020 🕐 Daily dinner; Mon–Fri Lunch 🚇 N, R, 4, 6 Union Square

NOBU (£££)

West Coast Americans had been thronging Nobu Matsuhisa's LA joint for some years before he opened in a TriBeCa bank. If only it still gave mortgages, so you could afford to order the chef's choice. Familiar *sushi*, *toro* (tuna) tartare, and similar slide between amazing creations that cost the earth, but may also move

it. Star restaurateur Drew Nieporent rules the *moderne* tables.

🔲 B11 ✉ 105 Hudson Street (Franklin Street) ☎ 212/219 0500 🕐 Mon–Sat dinner 🚇 1, 2, 3 Chambers Street

PATRIA (££–£££)

The South/Central America fusion ('Nuevo Latino') food of Doug Rodriguez is astonishing: mystery tubers (malanga, boniato); uncommon combos (banana-lentil salad); eye-poppingly bright flavours (coconut-glazed tuna with mango-onion-dried shrimp salsa); shocks (blue-cheese ice-cream). You can't understand it till you eat in this glam three-tiered place on the restaurant block of blocks.

🔲 D8 ✉ 250 Park Avenue South (20th Street) ☎ 212/777 6211 🕐 Closed Sun 🚇 N, R 23rd Street

UNION SQUARE CAFÉ (££–£££)

Danny Meyer is a restaurateur who feels the city's pulse with precision, and followed this Californian/Continental, vegetable-loving, seafood-heavy, bright, white, wooden-floored place with Gramercy Tavern (► 65). Kind and happy service, a tuna burger to die for, and veggies from heaven (there's a book about them) lead to virtual perfection.

🔲 C8 ✉ 21 E16th Street ☎ 212/243 4020 🕐 Closed Sun lunch 🚇 N, R, 4, 6 Union Square

A good deal

The Four Seasons' "Grill at Night" deal is one way to get a lot for less. Here are more: Daniel's (► 64), and Lutèce's (see left) set lunches; the '21' post-theatre supper; the bar menu at Union Square Café (► 64) or Gramercy Tavern (► 66) and the Cub Room Café (► 66); the lunch at Gotham (► 64); and – the New Yorker's favorite – the annual summer promotion whereby scores of the city's best restaurants offer a *prix fixe* set to reflect the year: during June of the millennium, lunch at Le Cirque 2000 (see left) will cost $20.00.

VENERABLE & EVERLASTING

What shall we eat tonight?

When you live in New York, responses to the dilemma include: Mexican, South-western, Cajun, Southern, Italian, French, Spanish, Japanese, Chinese, Vietnamese, Caribbean, Brazilian, Cuban, Chino-Latino, Jewish, Polish, Hungarian, Ukrainian, Greek, Irish, British, Austrian, Swedish, Thai, Korean, Indonesian, Malaysian, Indian, Peruvian, Tibetan, Burmese, Ethiopian, Afghan, Lebanese or Moroccan food. Even American. In New York you soon get familiar with every national and regional cuisine, as well as most permutations of hybrid.

CAFÉ DES ARTISTES (££–£££)

A Lincoln Center beauty and romantic date place, this classic is reminiscent of a grand boulevard brasserie, from the fine French menu to the naughty nude nymph murals. Sun-filled by day, candlelit at night, it's hard to dislike – and harder still for a sweet-toothed person who orders the famous dessert-tasting plate.
➕ E3 ✉ 1 W67th Street (Central Park West/Columbus Avenue) ☎ 212/877 3500 🕐 Daily 🚇 1, 9 66th Street

ELAINE'S (££)

At one time more celebs crammed into Elaine Kaufman's Italian Upper East Sider than cream in a cannoli. Now, according to *New York Magazine*'s schmoozy foodie, Gael Greene, they – Raquel Welch? Christian Slater? – are back. (Woody Allen never lets, since he and Elaine are proper friends.) Elaine and her pals are the only attraction – it's dark, the food is poor, and no one will notice *you*.
➕ H3 ✉ 1703 Second Avenue (88–89th Streets) ☎ 212/534 8103 🕐 Daily till late 🚇 4, 6 86th Street

OYSTER BAR (££)

The only thing New York has in common with a French provincial town is that its railway terminal shelters a great restaurant. It's in two parts: the vaulted, Guastavino-tiled bar, where you can sit at check-clothed tables or perch to order rounds of bivalves on the half-shell (don't even try to converse lunchtimes); and the wood-panelled wine bar, which is lovely and frumpy. Serves many oyster adjuncts.
➕ E6 ✉ Grand Central Terminal lower level ☎ 212/490 6650 🕐 Closed weekends 🚇 4, 5, 6, 7, 42nd Street, Grand Central

PETER LUGER (£££)

If you gotta have steak, big steak, and you don't want too many fellow tourists near, and you don't care about fresh greens or bowing and scraping, and you'd rather use cash than plastic, and you like a bit of history with dinner – this is where to go. It's been here since 1887, and only takes the Peter Luger card. Porterhouse lovers rate this the best in town.
➕ E6 ✉ 178 Broadway (Bedford Avenue) ☎ 718/387 7400 🕐 Daily 🚇 4, 6, 7 42nd Street

THE '21' CLUB (£££)

In the 1920s, when '21' was *the* speakeasy, it must have been a blast, but now, this dark bar-room restaurant, with its line of plaster jockeys on the front, is half tourist trap (ceiling crammed with toys, obsequious waiters, souvenir shop), half bankers' power canteen. It still packs a thrill for being so famous, though, and the food – burgers, game, lobster, steak – has been spring-cleaned and is good. You pay through the nose, except for the pre-5:30, post-10:30PM *prix fixe*.
➕ E5 ✉ 21 W52nd Street (Fifth/Sixth Avenues) ☎ 212/582 7200 🕐 Mon–Sat 🚇 B, D, F 47–50th Street

SCENES

BELL CAFFE (£)

A mini club scene has sprouted on the western-most blocks of SoHo's Spring Street, with this eclectic, organic café serving as central hangout. The crowds meld into the jumble of assorted chairs and colours, spilling on to the cobblestones in summer.

✚ B10 ✉ 310 Spring Street (Hudson Street) ☎ 212/334 2355 🕐 Daily till late 🚇 A, C Spring Street

BOWERY BAR (£–££)

There's always a single white-hot place which absorbs the full deck of models, fashion hags, mag eds, Eurotrash and artistes, and this was it when it opened, long ago. A barn-sized former gas station with forecourt garden in an unsavoury part of town, it still serves its roasted veg and caesar with chicken to people who like a crowd scene at dinner.

✚ C10 ✉ 358 Bowery (4th Street) ☎ 212/475 2220 🕐 Daily till late 🚇 6 Astor Place

CUB ROOM (£–£££)

This brick-walled, glass-fronted restaurant, bar and café is a magnet for a precisely defined stratum of well-heeled, good-look-ing, youthful professional. Ex-Lutèce sous-chef Henry Meer is in charge of the kitchen (roasted saged squab on ratatouille; soufflé for dessert).

✚ B10 ✉ 131 Sullivan Street ☎ 212/677 4100. Café: ✚ C10 ✉ 183 Prince Street ☎ 212/777 0030 🕐 Daily dinner; weekends lunch 🚇 N, R Prince Street

44 (££)

The joke about this Philippe Starck-designed catwalk of a restaurant in one of the city's most glam hostelries is that it's the staff canteen for Condé Nast and *New Yorker* editors. Only it's not a joke, because it's true, although many have defected to Michael's down the block. Food is balanced, leafy, exquisite.

✚ D6 ✉ The Royalton Hotel, 44 W44th Street (Fifth/Sixth Avenues) ☎ 212/944 8844 🕐 Daily 🚇 B, D, F 42nd Street

GRAMERCY TAVERN (££–£££)

This is Danny Meyer's (of Union Square Café ➤ 63) second place, and it's equally good. Armani-wearing waiters are so nice you nearly invite them to share Tom Colicchio's seasonal East Coast food (smoked duck 'pastrami', roasted rockfish with Manila clam sauce).

✚ D8 ✉ 42 E20th Street (Broadway/Park Avenues) ☎ 212/ 477 0777 🕐 Mon–Sat dinner; Mon–Fri lunch 🚇 6 23rd Street

LUCKY CHENG'S (£)

Past its first flush of attention, this East Village place, being unique, packs 'em in every night. The lighter-than-usual Californian-inflected Chinese food is surprising-ly good considering everyone goes to Lucky Cheng's for the waitresses: they're beautiful Asian drag queens, every one.

✚ D10 ✉ 24 First Avenue (1st/2nd Streets) ☎ 212/473 0516 🕐 Daily dinner 🚇 F 2nd Avenue

A strange year

1996 to 1997 was a strange year in the big ticket New York dining world. One by one the best-known tables in town were cleared, moved and not laid again for months. Missing from this edition, but back in town by now are Bouley, the top-ranked kitchen of star chef David Bouley, and the Russian Tea Room, the hokey, historic pseudo-Tsar's hangout. Le Cirque had just moved, the '21' Club had a new chef, and the maître d' and chef from the Odeon had just defected to the Independent.

NEIGHBOURHOOD FAVOURITES

Noshing

Although you will probably be able to understand most menus, New York cuisine (see panel on page 64 for what this constitutes) is so varied you are bound to encounter the odd problem. We hope this will help:

Arugula Roquette; still in everything

Bagel NY's are the best: chewy bread ring, boiled before it's baked

Bialy Crusty bagel-esque roll, with toasted onion centre

Bigos Hunter's stew, based on sauerkraut and kielbasa (Polish)

Blintz Crêpe rolled round fruit and sweet cheese (Jewish)

Burrito Soft tortilla with refried beans, beef, cheese, guacamole, sour cream (Mexican)

Cannoli Pastry tube with sweet ricotta cream; addictive (Italian)

Cha siu bao Steamed pork buns, *dim sum* (Cantonese)

Challah Braided egg bread, the best stuff for French toast (Jewish)

Chè ba màu Dessert of kidney beans, green jelly and coconut milk (Vietnamese)

Chilli relleno Green chilli stuffed with cheese, fried in batter (Mexican)

BRASSERIE (£–££)
The best features of this utterly *faux*-French, um, brasserie are that it's in the Mies van der Rohe Seagram Building, which is in a part of Midtown not rich in options, that it is dependable, inexpensive and that it never closes.
✚ F6 ⊠ 100 E53rd Street (Park/Lexington Avenues) ☎ 212/751 4840 ◉ 24 hours ⊕ 6 51st Street

EL TEDDY'S (£–££)
The actual-size Statue of Liberty crown on the awning, the crazy-colour mosaics, the premium margaritas, shaken not blenderised – these mark out El Teddy's from the Mexican pack, as does the menu's verve (no heart-burn burritos). Crazed with office refugees at weekends.
✚ B11 ⊠ 219 W Broadway (White Street) ☎ 212/941 7070 ◉ Daily till late ⊕ 1, 9 Franklin Street

EMPIRE DINER (£–££)
Deep in Chelsea near the river is this metallic ultra-diner (though it's candle – not neon – lit), serving meatloaf, sandwiches, pies and salads to an assortment of types, mostly trendy.
✚ B7 ⊠ 210 Tenth Avenue (22nd Street) ☎ 212/243 2736 ◉ 24 hours ⊕ C, E 23rd Street

FANELLI'S (£)
Dear tin-ceilinged, yellowing, draughty Fanelli's is the neighbourhood bar-restaurant all neighbourhoods should include. Despite its being well over a century old, it fails to charge a premium for the seasoning of history – not that it ought to for homely dishes (pasta, chilli, sandwiches, a prize burger) and brusque service.
✚ C10 ⊠ 94 Prince Street (Mercer Street) ☎ 212/226 9412 ◉ Daily, 10–late ⊕ N, R Prince Street

JERRY'S (£–££)
Looking like the diner of your dreams in red naughahyde, zebra stripes and spotlights, this SoHo haunt serves comfort dishes like half a roast chicken with garlic mash, roast veggies, pastas and salads. Upper West branch mimics the downtown cool.
✚ C10 ⊠ 101 Prince Street (Greene/Mercer Streets) ☎ 212/ 966 9464 ⊠ 302 Columbus Avenue (74/75th Streets) ☎ 212/501 7500 ◉ Closed Sun evening ⊕ N, R Prince Street

ODEON (£–££)
Arty people in this art deco TriBeCa space relax when fed with simple American-Parisian brasserie dishes: oyster fritters, blackened salmon with tomatillo sauce, grilled lamb shanks, profiteroles. It has weathered fashion.
✚ B11 ⊠ 145 W Broadway (Thomas Street) ☎ 212/233 0507 ◉ Daily till late ⊕ 1, 2, 3 Chambers Street

O'NEALS' (£–££)
So convenient for the Lincoln Center, though the eating's patchy: black bean soup and seared spicy shrimp are on the menu, but the burgers are best.
✚ D4 ⊠ 49 W64th Street (Broadway) ☎ 212/787 4663 ◉ Daily till late ⊕ 1, 2, 3, 9 66th Street

OUTDOORS, VIEWS, PEOPLE-WATCHING

BOATHOUSE CAFÉ (£–££)

The best thing to have at this Central Park zoo is the delicious lake view, but on most tables in summer can be seen the fruit and cheese platter. Once you've elbowed your way to a seat (the queuing system is flawed), you might follow suit, since the Italian menu is average.

✚ F3 ✉ East Park Drive (73rd Street) ☎ 212/517 2233 ◷ Closed Dec–Feb Ⓜ 6 68th Street

CAFFÈ DANTE (£)

Of the several Greenwich Village tiny-round-table Italians, this one is pleasing for the way you can get a prime sidewalk position when Reggio (at 119) is full – and superior pastries and gelati.

✚ B10 ✉ 79 MacDougal Street (Bleecker Street) ☎ 212/982 5275 ◷ Daily till late Ⓜ A, B, C, D, E, F W4th Street

LE JARDIN BISTRO (££)

The gorgeous grapevine-shaded garden is justifiably super-popular on a summer's evening, or for a family brunch. The French menu is acceptably homely.

✚ C11 ✉ 25 Cleveland Place ☎ 212/343–9599 ◷ Daily Ⓜ 6 Spring Street

LUNA PARK (£)

The Italian-ish food is oh-so-average, and the service is not brilliant, but this young and funky outdoors-only café in Union Square is great for a casual summer evening's supper. It is closed all winter.

✚ D9 ✉ Union Square Pavilion, 16th Street ☎ 212/475–8464 ◷ Closed Oct–Mar Ⓜ L, N, R, 4, 6 Union Square

MIRACLE GRILL (£)

Secreted behind East Village tenements is the prettiest garden and a restaurant pitched above the neighbourhood average. South-western is the style – broiled fish, chicken, shrimp, fruit salsas, salads and the best slushy, frozen strawberry margaritas.

✚ D10 ✉ 112 First Avenue (6/7th Streets) ☎ 212/254 2353 ◷ Daily dinner; weekends brunch Ⓜ 6 Astor Place

RAINBOW ROOM (£–£££)

Several options here at the 'view of views' run from a push-the-boat-out dinner dance extravaganza at 'Rainbow & Stars' to martinis with mixed nuts at the bar.

✚ E5 ✉ GE Building, 65th Floor, 30 Rockefeller Plaza (49/50th Streets) ☎ 212/632 5100 ◷ Tue–Sun dinner Ⓜ B, D, F 47–50th Street

TAVERN ON THE GREEN (£££)

Shamelessly, glitteringly out-of-towny (in every sense) is this fanciful fairy palace in Central Park, where every native child celebrates some rite of passage and foreigners hold PR launches.

✚ E4 ✉ Central Park West (67th Street) ☎ 212/873 3200 ◷ Daily Ⓜ 1, 9 66th Street

Chirashi Assorted raw fish on *sushi* rice (Japanese)

Chowder Creamy rich seafood soup; Manhattan's is tomato based

Cilantro Coriander leaf; used in everything

Clam sauce Red (tomatoey) or white (wine, cream) (Italian)

Deli As a cuisine: pastrami on rye, sauerkraut, Dr Brown's soda and the like (Jewish)

Dim sum Cantonese dumplings, buns and other little dishes

Egg cream Chocolate syrup, milk, carbonated water; no egg, no cream

Enchilada Like a burrito, but folded and baked (Mexican)

Gyro Broiled mystery meat, served in pitta, with salad

Half-sours Bright green cucumbers pickled with garlic (Jewish)

Hijiki Black tendrils of seaweed, cooked (organic places; Japanese)

Kielbasa Cured, meaty, spiced pork sausage (Polish)

Knish Thin pastry, thick potato, kasha, cheese, fruit filling (Jewish)

Latte Short coffee, long hot milk – one of many permutations

Lox Smoked salmon – with cream cheese it's the best bagel filling

DELI, PIZZA, BAGELS, BRUNCH

Maki Roll of *sushi* rice with filling wrapped in seaweed (Japanese)

Marinara Tomato, onion, garlic and herbs – your basic red sauce (Italian)

Napoleon Layers of pastry, cream, sometimes fruit (Italian)

Pho Vietnamese soups: clear broth with beef and vegetables

Pierogi Pasta pillows of potato, meat or cheese, boiled or fried (Polish)

Pignoli Pine nuts, or little pine-nut-crusted cookies or tarts (Italian)

Pretzel New York's are soft-centred and sea-salted, and are sold from carts

Rugelach Tiny, buttery rolled pastries with dried fruit (Jewish)

Sashimi Just the raw fish part of *sushi*

Schmear Thin smear of cream cheese for bagel use (Jewish)

Sfogliatella Shell-shaped ribbed pastry, filled with sweet ricotta (Italian)

Slice Of pizza. Best in the world

Sushi Raw fish on a mound of vinegared rice (Japanese)

Tamale Stuffed cornmeal roll, wrapped in corn husk and steamed (Mexican)

Verjus Wine by-product, predicted to be in everything now

CARNEGIE DELI (£–££)
Known to have the rudest waiters, and the biggest sandwiches. It was the one in *Broadway Danny Rose*.
⊞ E5 ⊠ 854 Seventh Avenue (54–55th Streets) ☎ 212/757 2245 ⏰ Closed Sat 🚇 N, R 57th Street

KATZ'S DELI (£)
The fake orgasm scene in *When Harry Met Sally*; signs saying 'Send a salami to your boy in the army'; professionally rude countermen (tip for a fatter sandwich)...It's an 1888 landmark.
⊞ D11 ⊠ 205 E Houston Street (Ludlow Street) ☎ 212/254 2246 ⏰ Closed Sat 🚇 F Second Avenue

LOMBARDI'S (£)
No new coal-fired pizza ovens (essential for the correct slightly charred, crisp crust) are allowed to be built in New York, so the owner of this tiny café tracked down the grandson of the original Lombardi (Gennaro, thought to have made NY's first *ever* pizza in 1905), and revived his disused one. It still makes great pies.
⊞ C11 ⊠ 32 Spring Street (Mott Street) ☎ 212/941 7994 ⏰ Daily 🚇 6 Spring Street

RAY'S PIZZA (£)
Every pizza joint in town is called Ray's Original or Famous Original Ray's or Original Ray's Famous, except this one. Can you guess? This *is* the original Ray's – or the one with the best claim.
⊞ C11 ⊠ 27 Prince Street (Mott Street) ☎ 212/966 1960 ⏰ Closed Sun evening 🚇 6 Spring Street

ROYAL CANADIAN PANCAKE HOUSE (£)
'Pancakes make people happy' says the sign, succinctly. Over 50 fillings go into the frisbee-sized monsters. (Two branches.)
⊞ F6 ⊠ 1004 Second Avenue (53rd Street) ☎ 212/980 4131 ⏰ Daily 🚇 6 51st Street

SARABETH'S (£)
There are outposts in the Hotel Wales and the Whitney, which says something about the class of this simple wholesome food operation. It's the bakery that thrills, though.
⊞ E2 ⊠ 423 Amsterdam Avenue (80th/81st Streets) ☎ 212/ 496 6280 ⏰ Daily 🚇 1, 9 79th Street

SERENDIPITY 3 (£–££)
The ice-cream parlour you longed for as a child, filled with toys and serving desserts that block out the person opposite. Famous for the dangerous Frozen Hot Chocolate, made with 14 different imported kinds.
⊞ F5 ⊠ 225 E60th Street (Second /Third Avenues) ☎ 212/ 838 3531 ⏰ Daily till midnight 🚇 4, 6 39th Street

SYLVIA'S (£)
Sylvia's has surpassed institution status and made it into the industry bracket, but it is still the essential Harlem stop – especially for the Gospel Brunch, when the fried chicken and corn-bread comes with live singers.
⊞ Off map at H1 ⊠ 328 Lennox Avenue (126th/127th Streets) ☎ 212/996 0660 ⏰ Mon– Sat 🚇 2, 3 125th Street

ASIAN: PHO TO *SUSHI*

BO KY (£)

The phrase 'no frills' doesn't do justice to the ugly formica interior, but the 20-odd noodle soups are both restorative and delicious, and the price of a magazine.

🔲 C11 ✉ 80 Bayard Street (Mott Street) ☎ 212/406 2292 🕐 Daily 🚇 N, R Canal Street

JAPONICA (£–££)

Long, long ago, *sushi* was fashionable. Nowadays, exquisite arrangements of raw fish on rice are merely one of many things to have for dinner. Japonica is the favourite of a great many people, so go off-peak. There's *tempura*, *teriyaki* and so on for the squeamish.

🔲 C9 ✉ 100 University Place (12th Street) ☎ 212/243 7752 🕐 Daily 🚇 N, R, 4, 6 Union Square

KELLEY & PING (£)

Fake Chinatown, with styling that dispenses with the tiresome fluorescent lights in favour of hopsack, candles and bare wood. Serves satisfying spicy noodle dishes to yuppie artists and Angelika movie-house patrons.

🔲 C10 ✉ 127 Greene Street (Houston Street) ☎ 212/228 1212 🕐 Daily 🚇 B, D, F Broadway/Lafayette Street

KOM TANG SOOT BUL HOUSE (£)

This Korean barbeque place would be worth patronising for its name alone, but the cook-at-table, red meat feasting style is fun, and this place does it well.

🔲 D7 ✉ 32 W32nd Street (Fifth Avenue)

☎ 212/947 8482 🕐 Daily 🚇 B, D, F, N, R 34th Street

NEW YORK NOODLETOWN (£)

Hong Kong in miniature. Have salt-baked soft-shell crab, caramelised beef with noodles, jumbo shrimp with black pepper sauce. It's all good, and the price of a sandwich.

🔲 C11 ✉ 281/2 Bowery (Bayard Street) ☎ 212/349 0923 🕐 Daily 🚇 F East Broadway

PHO PASTEUR (£)

Opposite the jailhouse, a satisfying Vietnamese place, stark of décor, bright of light, but with a novella-length menu and fabulous phood. (Nha Trang, at 87, is just as good, if this is full.)

🔲 C11 ✉ 85 Baxter Street (Mulberry Street) ☎ 212/608 3656 🕐 Daily 🚇 N, R Canal Street

SHABU-SHABU EAST (£)

Japanese that surpasses sushi for entertainment. You get a pile of veg, a plate of wafer-thin meat or fish, and each diner has his own pot of simmering stock to cook it all.

🔲 F5 ✉ 235 W55th Street ☎ 212/246 2808 🕐 Daily 🚇 6 51st Street

TWENTY MOTT STREET (£)

One of the most popular dim sum palaces that also does a mean glossily caramelised roast duck. Despite three floors, it's war here on Sundays.

🔲 C12 ✉ 20 Mott Street (Bowery) ☎ 212/964 0380 🕐 Daily 🚇 F East Broadway

Wasabi Virulent green, ultra-hot horseradish condiment (Japanese)

Yogurt Frozen yoghurt. Euphemism for ice-cream

Zeppole Type of doughnut (Italian)

Giant *sushi*

For the *sushi* connoisseur, Yama (£–££) may not offer the best there is, but it does serve the biggest *sushi* and it is very good. Sadly, many people share this view, and the tiny place is engulfed by salivating *sushi* wolves, lining up for hours.

🔲 D9 ✉ 49 Irving Place (17th Street)

☎ 212/475–0969 🕐 Closed Sun 🚇 N, R, 4, 5, 6 14 Street Union Square

NEIGHBOURHOODS/STREETS

New York shopping rules

As well as being a restaurant expert, each New Yorker is a shopping oracle on legs. The following laws obtain:

1) Never pay retail.
2) If in doubt, take it back.
3) So know the returns policy.
4) Buy it now. It'll be gone later.
5) Buy cheap, buy twice.
6) Remember purchase tax: it is not included on the price ticket, and can be reclaimed later by non-US citizens.

CANAL STREET

The Chinatown main drag is the irresistibly gaudy source of fakes: bad copies of Gucci and Rolex watches, Chanel-like bags, Hermès-esque scarves from West Broadway to Mott Street, plus bargain stores of electrical appliances, trainers, telephones...Real bargains are possible, however – and check out Pearl Paint (➤ 76) and the exotic Pearl River Mart (➤ 71).
🚇 B11 🚊 N, R Canal Street

FIFTH AVENUE

Stroll from Rockefeller to the Park for swanky window-shopping or a heavy workout for your plastic. Talk to Harry Winston! Have breakfast at Tiffany's! Some designers (clothes) are here, the rest on Madison; also find Saks, Bergdorf's, Bendel's, FAO Schwarz (toys; ➤ 57) and tacky Trump Tower.
🚇 D7–F4 🚊 6 59th Street

57TH STREET

Fiendishly priced antiques, and one-off shops, from the Warner Bros Studio Store to Chanel and from Prada to Laura Ashley, all interspersed with theme restaurants (Planet Hollywood et al). Bloomingdale's is near by.
🚇 D5–F5 🚊 N, R 57th Street

HERALD SQUARE

Mainly for Macy's. Also here is tacky K-Mart.
🚇 D7 🚊 B, D, F, N, R 34th Street

LOWER BROADWAY

NY University students' mecca for vintage clothing, boots, boots, boots (also 8th Street to Sixth Avenue) and Tower Records (➤ 74).
🚇 C10 🚊 B, D, F Broadway Lafayette

MADISON AVENUE

Synonymous with the advertising industry, but also with the smartest top shops: Italians Gucci, Versace, Armani, Missoni, Valentino; Americans Ralph Lauren, Coach; and Barneys. Other notables – Crate & Barrel, Calvin Klein – have followed Barney's lead.
🚇 E6–F4 🚊 N, R 5th Avenue

ORCHARD STREET

Open every day bar the Jewish sabbath, but showing its best bazaar-like bustle on Sundays, the Lower East Side's artery has fashion, from tawdry trinkets to low-price designers.
🚇 D11 🚊 F Delancey Street

SOHO

The Cast-Iron Historic District once generated creative energy in former sweatshops converted into studios and galleries, but now generates mostly consumer lust. It's a high-rent retail enclave of galleries, fancy interiors stores, ethnic artefacts purveyors, Euro fashion houses, plus bars and restaurants.
🚇 B/C10 🚊 N, R Prince Street

UPPER WEST

This is boutique land, including repeats of downtown hits (Betsey Johnson, Sacco shoes...), and Zabar's (➤ 75).
🚇 E/F1/2 🚊 1, 9 79th Street

DEPARTMENT STORES

BARNEY'S

We all want to dress at top-dollar Barney's. Every designer's here, including loads of Europeans (even more coveted than home-growns like Karan, Beene, Mizrahi, Sui). Barney's was all menswear until the current Pressman family regenerated it, and although they then went bankrupt, they saved the store.

📍 C8 ✉ 106 Seventh Avenue (17th Street) ☎ 212/ 929 9000 ✉ A, C, E 14 Street ✉ 660 Madison Avenue (61st Street) ☎ 212/ 826 8900 🚇 N, R Lexington Avenue

BERGDORF GOODMAN

Even if it says so itself in the way it bills the Men's Store across the street, Bergdorf's is the ultimate. Snobs and nobs can feel at home, with Turnbull & Asser, Gidden's and Penhaligon's, plus many designers' collections displayed in palatial spaces.

📍 E5 ✉ 754 Fifth Avenue (57th Street) ☎ 212/ 753 7300 🚇 4, 6 59th Street

BLOOMINGDALES

Please don't call it Bloomies – it's glitzy enough already without this diminutive, though there are admittedly entire floors devoted to ceramic *objets* inscribed with that very word. Even wordless things scream for attention here, in the spiritual home of big hair.

📍 F5 ✉ 1000 Third Avenue (59th Street) ☎ 212/705 2000 🚇 4, 6 59th Street

LORD & TAYLOR

It's simply a lovely, rather old-fashioned store, of

manageable size and good for separates. Best of all are its Christmas window displays, which, with their animated figures, are a holiday tradition.

📍 D6 ✉ 424 Fifth Avenue (39th Street) ☎ 212/391 3344 🚇 4, 6 Grand Central

MACY'S

The most famous store in the world, partly thanks to movie exposure (principally *Miracle on 34th Street*, remade in 1994), but mainly to the fact that it's the BIGGEST store in the world. The quantity of merchandise is staggering: you can wear out shoe leather looking for the shoe department. Kitchenware in The Cellar is a highlight, as is the cosmetics floor.

📍 D7 ✉ 151 W34th Street (Herald Square) ☎ 212/695 4400 🚇 B, D, F, N, R 34th Street

SAKS FIFTH AVENUE

Despite the classy address (it's also in cities and resort towns nationwide), Saks is unsnooty and known for good service. Designer collections are dispersed in their own shoplets, and there's good menswear of a more conservative breed than Barney's.

📍 E6 ✉ 611 Fifth Avenue (50th Street) ☎ 212/753 4000 🚇 E, F 5th Avenue

TAKASHIMAYA

If you're seeking fat price tags, try this exquisite Japanese emporium, with its atrium gallery. The tea-room will 'Zen' you out of any shopping trauma.

📍 E5 ✉ 693 Fifth Avenue (55th Street) ☎ 212/350 0115 🚇 E, F 5th Avenue

Pearl River Mart

You can't see this Chinese department store from the street, despite the fact that it has three floors stuffed with stuff and two entrances. Shop here, in an atmosphere reminiscent of some household consumer shrine of the 1950s, for chrome lunch pails with clip-on lids; embroidered silk pyjamas and Suzy Wong dresses; bamboo fans and porcelain rice bowls – all the things, in fact, you can get in the smaller Chinatown emporia, but collected under one roof. The food department sells everything from dried squid and McVities Digestives. The prices are very, very low.

📍 B11 ✉ 277 Canal Street (Broadway) ☎ 212/431 4770 🚇 N, R Canal Street

CLOTHES

More shops

Agnès B
✉ 1063 Madison Avenue
☎ 212/570 9333

Armani Exchange
✉ 568 Broadway
☎ 212/431 6000

Chanel
✉ 5 E57th Street
☎ 212/355 5050

Comme des Garçons
✉ 116 Wooster Street
☎ 212/219 0660

Gianni Versace
✉ 817 Madison Avenue
☎ 212/744 6868

Gucci
✉ 685 Fifth Avenue
☎ 212/826 2600

Hermès
✉ 11 E57th Street
☎ 212/751 3181

Polo/Ralph Lauren
✉ 867 Madison Avenue (72nd
Street) ☎ 212/606 2100

Prada
✉ 45 E57th Street
☎ 212/308 2332

Timberland
✉ 709 Madison Avenue
☎ 212/754 0436

Yohji Yamamoto
✉ 103 Grand Street
☎ 212/966 9066

WOMEN'S

ANNA SUI
This is the woman who puts out velvet flares one year, then dayglo baby-doll dirndls the next. Silly, but revered and *loved*.
✚ C10 ✉ 113 Green Street
☎ 212/941 8406 🚇 N, R Prince Street

BETSEY JOHNSON
Madly coloured, usually very clingy downtown dressing-up clothes.
✚ E3 ✉ 248 Columbus Avenue (71st Street) and 130 Thompson Street ☎ 212/362 3364 🚇 1, 2, 3 72nd Street

J MORGAN PUETT
An unique, timeless aesthetic from this former sculptor, who hand-dyes linens, silks, cottons into cloud and earth colours and makes Amish-inspired shapes with them.
✚ C10 ✉ 140 Wooster Street
☎ 212/677 1200 🚇 N, R Prince Street

MORGANE LE FAY
Liliana Ordas's floaty, yet tailored, slightly theatrical clothes in strong, plain colours, and natural fibres. (Branch at 151 Spring Street, SoHo.)
✚ F3 ✉ 746 Madison Avenue (74th Street) ☎ 212/879 9700 🚇 6 77th Street

NICOLE MILLER
Girl-about-town Miller designs fun, fitted suits, frocks and accessories with tongue in cheek. Fabrics and finish don't always match the price tags. (Branch in SoHo.)
✚ F4 ✉ 780 Madison Avenue (66th Street) ☎ 212/288 9779 🚇 6 77th Street

MEN'S

BROOKS BROTHERS
The button-down shirts and khakis, the docksiders and plaid bermudas, the blazers...the Ivy look.
✚ E6 ✉ 346 Madison Avenue (45th Street) ☎ 212/682 8800 🚇 4, 6 Grand Central

TODAY'S MAN
All-purpose, good-value casual and formal wear in a gigantic shop. Lesser labels include the likes of Lauren and St Lauren.
✚ C8 ✉ 625 Sixth Avenue
☎ 212/924 0200 🚇 F 23rd Street

BOTH

BANANA REPUBLIC
For high street, this is good quality fashion, exactly half-way between Ralph Lauren and The Gap.
✚ C9 ✉ 89 Fifth Avenue
☎ 212/366 4691 🚇 L, N, R, 4, 6 Union Square

CANAL JEANS
T-shirts, plaid shirts, vintage frocks, cut-offs, most brands of denim, plus Carhart and CAT workwear, and their own multi-hued cottons.
✚ C10 ✉ 504 Broadway (Broome Street) ☎ 212/226 1130 🚇 N, R Prince Street

CHARIVARI
One of the best small chains anywhere, stocking carefully selected mono-chrome high-style, but not fashion-victim, separates. Call for branches.
✚ C8 ✉ 257 Columbus Avenue (72nd Street)
☎ 212/787 7272 🚇 1, 2, 3 72nd Street

CLOTHES FOR LESS

BIG STORES

CENTURY 21
This huge department store has an annoying lack of changing rooms except in 'European Designers', which is where the Gigli, Versace, Armani, Gaultier you wanted is anyway.
⊞ A12 ✉ 22 Cortlandt Street ☎ 212/227 9092 🚇 C, E World Trade Center

DAFFY'S
'Clothing Bargains for Millionaires' is the nonsensical motto of this three-branch chain. What they mean is: sift through acres of orange-sequinned polyester catsuits hoping you recognise the Jasper, even without the label. Good for casual stuff, too.
⊞ C8 ✉ 111 Fifth Avenue ☎ 212/529 4477 🚇 L, N, R, 4, 6 Union Square

WOMEN'S

ENCORE
Very close to Michael's, and similar, but this stocks some menswear too. Prices at both are not unrelated to the originals – we're talking hundreds, not tens.
⊞ G3 ✉ 1132 Madison Avenue ☎ 212/879 2850 🚇 6 77th Street

KLEIN'S OF MONTICELLO
A peacock among Lower East Side pigeons: mostly European designers.
⊞ D11 ✉ 105 Orchard Street ☎ 212/966 1453 🚇 F Delancey Street

MICHAEL'S RESALE
Being smack in the middle of spiffy Madison Avenue, you'd expect quality here, and you get it. After all, Upper East Side ladies don't touch anything without knowing its pedigree. Labels are along the Ferragamo, Ungaro, Valentino axis.
⊞ G3 ✉ 2nd Floor, 1041 Madison Avenue ☎ 212/737 7273 🚇 6 77th Street

MEN'S

MOE GINSBERG
This classic consignment (as opposed to seconds) store is very well known. There are five floors, well-trained salesmen, a tailor next door (alterations cost extra), and just about every label up to Calvin Klein, Hugo Boss and Saint Laurent level.
⊞ C8 ✉ 162 Fifth Avenue (21st Street) ☎ 212/242 3482 🚇 L, N, R, 4, 6 Union Square

BOTH

INA
Few showroom samples, but many delicious, slightly worn labels (Ina has an eye). Alaïa, Versace, Beene, Mugler, Armani are usually around. Ask for the other branch too.
⊞ C10 ✉ 101 Thompson Street (Prince Street) ☎ 212/941 4757 🚇 N, R Prince Street

OUT OF OUR CLOSET
Terin Fischer's tiny, spectacular consignment store includes current season samples from designers who make fashion fans salivate: Yohji, Dolce, Comme, Mugler, Gaultier, even Chanel.
⊞ C8 ✉ 136 W18th Street ☎ 212/633 6965 🚇 F 23rd Street

Thrift stores

Now that recycling is hot, so are these stores. The SoHo Salvation Army (✉ Spring Street at Lafayette Street) is a cult among low-budget film art directors, but thrift shops are still thickest on the Upper East Side. The Irvington Institute (✉ Second Avenue at 80th Street) and Spence Chapin (✉ Third Avenue at 80th Street) are especially big and fruitful. Also try Cancer Care (✉ Third Avenue at 83rd Street), Godmothers' League (✉ Third Avenue at 82nd Street), Memorial Sloane-Kettering (Third Avenue at 81st Street) and Call Again (✉ Second Avenue at 89th Street). Downtown a bit are a clutch more: The Calvary/St George's (✉ 208 E16th Street), in a church basement; Repeat Performance (✉ 220 E23rd Street), which benefits the City Opera; and Second Time Around, next door. Biggest is Brooklyn's Domsey Warehouse (✉ 431 Kent Avenue/496 Wythe Avenue ☎ 718/384 6000) with bewildering acres of work clothes, military wear, denims, prom dresses and vintage stuff sorted by era, plus a department where you pay by weight.

SUPERSTORES

Bigger, better

'New Yorkers don't need another boutique', the owner of nationwide housewares store Crate & Barrel declared just before his 54,000 square feet of midtown Manhattan debuted in early 1995. Regardless of whether New Yorkers agree with him, since the invasion of the superstores picked up speed they are indeed getting precious few boutiques. Will the big guys kill the corner deli? Most think not. New Yorkers are going to spend the cash anyway, so why not keep it in the city? And why shouldn't Manhattanites enjoy the up to 45 per cent discounts the rest of the country gets from superstores? After all, the city's been through it all before, with no harm done. The last age of giant department stores – including S Klein's, Wanamaker's, McCreery's, Bonwit Teller and Stern Brothers of Ladies' Mile – happened, spookily enough, during the closing years of the last century.

BARNES & NOBLE
Who would have predicted book shopping would become sexy? This phenomenon of – well, it's had to say of what – opened its huge Upper West Side self, complete with coffee bar, couches and events, in 1993, and won an instant reputation as a singles cruising arena. The Sixth Avenue branch followed, then Astor Place, then Union Square. B&N itself has been around since 1873.
✚ E2 ✉ 2289 Broadway (82nd Street) ☎ 212/362 8835 🚇 1, 9 79th Street

BED, BATH & BEYOND
This monster was the first to colonise Chelsea along Sixth Avenue, the neighbourhood of the giants. The name says it all. Come, see and be conquered.
✚ C8 ✉ 620 Sixth Avenue (19th Street) ☎ 212/255 3550 🚇 F 23rd Street

BRADLEES
Like a reincarnation of S Klein's-on-the-Square, crossed with the spirit of Woolworths, everything in this gigantic emporium is cheap, cheap, cheap – just like the countless gaudy stores along adjacent 14th Street.
✚ D9 ✉ Union Square ☎ 212/673 5814 🚇 L, N, R, 4, 6 Union Square

COMP USA
Possibly the most useful of all for the visitor, since it undercuts everyone and sells everything – wares hard and soft, modems, CD-ROM drives etc.
✚ D7 ✉ 420 Fifth Avenue (37th Street) ☎ 212/764 6224 🚇 B, D, F, N, R 34th Street

CRATE & BARREL
Having refreshed your wardrobe at the uptown Barney's, you can nip next door for the wardrobe itself, perhaps in cherrywood. C&B's stores are renowned for taste, value and variety.
✚ F5 ✉ Madison Avenue (59th Street) ☎ 212/308 0011 🚇 N, R 5th Avenue

NIKE TOWN N.Y.
You feel like an athlete on the winners' podium just striding into this futuristic dream drome.
✚ D6 ✉ 11 Pennsylvania Plaza (57th Streeet) ☎ 212/946–2710 🚇 N, R 57th Street

TODAY'S MAN (► 72)

TOWER RECORDS
The downtown superstore, with its book and video arms and Outlet, is credited with revitalising the entire area of 'NoHo' (north of Houston), because it's a youth magnet.
✚ C10 ✉ 692 Broadway (4th Street) ☎ 212/505 1500 🚇 B, D, F Broadway Lafayette

TOYS 'R' US
The supermarket for children. Two branches.
✚ D9 ✉ 24–32 Union Square East ☎ 212/674–8697 🚇 L, N, R, 4, 6 Union Square ✚ D7 ✉ 1293 Broadway (Herald Square) ☎ 212/594– 8697 🚇 B, D, F, N, R 34th Street

VIRGIN MEGASTORE
The British are coming.
✚ D6 ✉ 1540 Broadway ☎ 212/921 1020 🚇 N, R 42nd Street

FOOD

BALDUCCI'S

The first (alphabetically speaking) of the three Manhattan grocers that are so comprehensive, so beautifully laid out, so irresistibly stocked with things you want to devour, that you could designate them food museums. This Greenwich Village one is still owned by the family that started it as a stall across the street. The Balduccis, true to their origins, put the emphasis on Italian produce and irresistible prepared dishes (oh, the anchovy tart!).

✚ C9 ✉ 424 Sixth Avenue (9th Street) ☎ 212/673 2600 Ⓜ A, B, C, D, E, F W4th Street

DEAN & DELUCA

The loft-like, mosaic-floored, all-white, vast space gives centre stage to the cornucopia. Every foodstuff has its own little gallery: piles of cookies; towers of spices in tiny chrome canisters; baskets of onion ficelles, rosemary focaccia, rye, seven-grain, brioches; fresh fish, cheese, pasta; copper pans, cookbooks – *everything*. Unfortunately, standards have dropped since the owners sold up.

✚ C10 ✉ 560 Broadway (Prince Street) ☎ 212/431 8350 Ⓜ N, R Prince Street

GOURMET GARAGE

GG started as a wholesale outlet for baby veg/olive oil/coffee beans, etc, run by some NYC culinary networkers. Now it's the place to find yellow cherry tomatoes, dried cherries, fresh clams, truffle butter, smoked duck, smoked trout, *gelati*, you-name-it,

and it only *acts* like it's bargain-priced. Pick up the *GG Gazette* with your lunch at the deli counter.

✚ B11 ✉ 435 Broome Street (Mercer Street) ☎ 212/941 5850 Ⓜ N, R Prince Street

RUSS & DAUGHTERS

This, being a true New York 'appetising deli', would wither and die outside the city or even many blocks north. Devotees travel blocks and blocks for the lox, carp, smoked whitefish, pickled herrings, and so on.

✚ D11 ✉ 179 E Houston Street (Orchard Street) ☎ 212/475 4880 Ⓜ F 2nd Avenue

YONAH SCHIMMEL

The companion piece to the Russ & Daughters, and only a few blocks west, this remarkable, scrappy-looking anachronism is said to serve the best fruit, cheese, kasha, and potato knishes in New York (and thus in the world).

✚ D11 ✉ 137 E Houston Street ☎ 212/477 2858 Ⓜ F 2nd Avenue

ZABAR'S

This is the most wisecracking of the three Manhattan grocers, just as big and bustling and produce-packed, but with such a different soul. Here's where you pick up the ultimate half sours, bagels, Nova lox, babka, rugelach and such. Shopping here makes you think about how you'll get it all on the plate, not about what the plate will look like, as at D&D.

✚ E2 ✉ 2245 Broadway (80th Street) ☎ 212/787 2000 Ⓜ 1, 9 79th Street

Picnic spots

These don't start and end in Central Park. Some more to try, indoors and out:

Lower Manhattan Battery Park City – benches and views all along the Hudson South Street Seaport boardwalk

SoHo The 'Vest Pocket Park' at Spring and Mulberry Streets, and the playground outside Coles Sports Center, Mercer and Houston Streets

Greenwich Village The ballpark at Clarkson and Hudson Streets, and St Luke's Garden at Hudson (Barrow/Grove Streets) are a well-kept secret – they're perfect! Union Square Park for the Greenmarket

Midtown East Greenacre Park at 51st Street and Second Avenue (what a misnomer). New York Public Library steps or tables at Bryant Park. Crystal Pavilion (Third Avenue/50th Street) atrium with waterfall, and Paley Park (53rd Street/Fifth Avenue) concrete canyon with waterfall

Midtown West Equitable Tower Atrium on Seventh Avenue, 51st–52nd streets – greenery!

Upper East Side Carl Schurz Park, East End Avenue, 84–89th streets. Gracie Mansion, where the mayor lives is here, also great Roosevelt Island and bridge views.

NOWHERE BUT NEW YORK

Summertime

You know it's summer when the block fairs descend. Every Sunday, at least one Manhattan block of blocks sprouts a forest of police hurdles, and the air thickens with the distinctive aroma of frying zeppole and bratwurst. At first, these collections of stalls are charm itself, but after a while they begin to look samey: the same stalls with the same hand-painted batik leather-thonged jackets; the same troupe of Andean nose-flautists flogging copies of their CD; the same person eating the same falafel. This is no less true if you pass two on the same day, since they are able to clone at will. It would be a benign phenomenon if unscrupulous entrepreneurs didn't cream all the profits, but they do. There are better things to do on a Sunday.

GOOD GIFTS

CASWELL-MASSEY

If your hotel's a fancy one, chances are they stocked your bathroom with smellies from here.
✚ E6 ✉ 518 Lexington Avenue ☎ 212/755 2254
🚇 6 51th Street

ENCHANTED FOREST

Children have to be taken to this aptly named grotto of stuffed animals and fairytale things.
✚ C10 ✉ 85 Mercer Street
☎ 212/925 6677 🚇 N, R Prince Street

FIREFIGHTER'S FRIEND

Yes, it's the NYFD's shop, selling the essential souvenirs: 'Keep Back 200-Ft' T-shirts and metal-clamp-fastened oilskins, long purloined by the fashion crowd.
✚ C10 ✉ 263 Lafayette Street ☎ 212/226 3142 🚇 6 Spring

GUGGENHEIM MUSEUM STORE

From investment pieces to trinkets, and all in the best possible, most modern taste.
✚ C10 ✉ 575 Broadway
☎ 212/423 3875 🚇 N, R Prince Street

KATE'S PAPERIE

A paper shop dull? Try this, and weep. Many paper-related *objets* too. (Another on 10th Street.)
✚ C10 ✉ 561 Broadway
☎ 212/941 9816 🚇 N, R Prince Street

M.A.C.

Women (and drag queens) who wear any make-up at all, ever, ought to know this cult range of pigment-rich cosmetics. It employs RuPaul and kd lang as its 'Spokesmodels'.
✚ C9 ✉ 14 Christopher Street
☎ 212/243 4150 🚇 A, B, C, D, E, F W4th Street

PEARL PAINT

Rock-bottom priced art supplies, craft materials, stationery, frames, etc.
✚ B11 ✉ 308 Canal Street (Broadway) ☎ 212/431 7932
🚇 N, R Canal Street

THE STRAND

More a way of life than a bookstore: it's easy to get lost in its '8 miles' of secondhand and remaindered books and half-price review copies. They do searches.
✚ C9 ✉ 828 Broadway
☎ 212/473 1452 🚇 N, R, 4, 6 Union Square

HOME

BROADWAY PANHANDLER

One of the most comprehensive kitchen supply stores, and one of the best priced; wares good enough for the semi-pro.
✚ C10 ✉ 477 Broome Street
☎ 212/966 3434 🚇 N, R Prince Street

PRATESI

Fabulous costly linens.
✚ F4 ✉ 829 Madison Avenue (69th Street) ☎ 212/288 2315
🚇 6 68th Street

SOHO MILL

Bargain linens, mostly seconds from major ranges. Especially good for towels.
✚ C10 ✉ 490 Broadway, 2nd Floor ☎ 212/226 8040 🚇 N, R Prince Street

WOLFMAN-GOLD & GOOD

This pioneer of all SoHo's million interior-designers stores is still the leader of trends in tabletops.

📍 C10 ✉ 117 Mercer Street ☎ 212/431 1888 🚇 N, R Prince Street

STRANGE

ASTOR PLACE HAIRSTYLISTS

More of a theatre than a store. Many a famous head's been shorn here.

📍 C9 ✉ 2 Astor Place ☎ 212/475 9854 🚇 6 Astor Place

CHARLES' PLACE INC

Charles Elkaim forges flamboyant, fun jewellery out of miniatures and rhinestones. He also sells doll's-house furniture and mint vintage toy cars.

📍 C10 ✉ 234 Mulberry Street ☎ 212/966 7302 🚇 6 Spring Street

THE EROTIC BAKER

The name is no lie. Get a fudge-frosted phallus here. Special orders take 24 hours.

📍 E1 ✉ 582 Amsterdam Avenue (88th Street) ☎ 212/362 7557 🚇 1, 9 86th Street

THE FAN CLUB

Do you feel the need to own Dolly Parton's blouse? Audrey Hepburn's slacks? Here they are, for real.

📍 C8 ✉ 22 W19th Street ☎ 212/929 3349 🚇 1, 2, 3 14th Street

SILLY

LITTLE RICKIE'S

A retirement home for the novelty items of five decades: glue-on beauty marks, ant farms, wind-up teeth and excellent cards.

📍 D10 ✉ 491/2 First Avenue (3rd Street) ☎ 212/505 6467 🚇 F 2nd Avenue

LOVE SAVES THE DAY

This – ostensibly a vintage clothes store – is crammed with mauve circus spangles, 1950s Barbies, Cliff Richard disguise kits, Elvis wigs – you get the picture. Rosanna Arquette bought Madonna's jacket here in *Desperately Seeking Susan*.

📍 D10 ✉ 119 Second Avenue ☎ 212/228 3802 🚇 F 2nd Avenue

WEIRD

MAXILLA & MANDIBLE

Bones are the basic merchandise here, with related butterflies, shells and antlers.

📍 E2 ✉ 453 Columbus Avenue (81st Street) ☎ 212/724 6173 🚇 C 81th Street

PANDORA'S BOX

It's hard to move for the plaster cherubs, Nefertitis, columns and, wherever you look, an Elvis.

📍 B10 ✉ 153 Prince Street ☎ 212/505 7615 🚇 C, E Spring Street

PARACELSO

'I have exquisite taste' says Luxor, who has blue eyebrows and hails from Milan. Her store beams with cloth of gold, sequins, striped chiffons and velvets, like a magpie's nest.

📍 B10 ✉ 414 W Broadway ☎ 212/966 4232 🚇 C, E Spring Street

Flea markets

In a city whose best junk shops are more interested in hiring out pieces for filmset dressing than selling them, flea markets flourish. The prime flea is the Annex (✉ Sixth Avenue at 26th Street ☎ 212/243 5343 🕐 Sat–Sun), long established, antique-y and huge, with a small charge for admission. Second is the far newer, but similar, SoHo (✉ Broadway at Grand Street ☎ 212/682 2000 🕐 Sat–Sun). The Annex has an adjunct, the Garage (✉ 112 W25th Street ☎ 212/647 0707 🕐 Sat, Sun), which isn't a real flea because it's indoors. Two uptown markets include crafts and greenmarket stalls among the antiques and bric-à-brac: the I.S. 44 Green Flea (✉ Columbus Avenue at 77th Street ☎ 212/721 0900 🕐 Sun), and the inside-outside P.S. 183 (✉ E67th Street at York Avenue 🕐 Sat).

BARS & COFFEE BARS

Cocktails

Think very dry martinis with an olive rather than scarlet alcoholic slushpuppies. Where to order one?

LOUNGE BARS

Fez

✉ 380 Lafayette Street
☎ 212/533 2680

Pravda

✉ 281 Lafayette Street
☎ 212/226–4696

Merc Bar

✉ 151 Mercer Street
☎ 212/966 2727

Temple Bar

✉ 332 Lafayette Street
☎ 212/925 4242

SKYLINE GRAZING

Top of the Sixes

✉ 666 Fifth Avenue
☎ 212/757 6662

Rainbow Room (▶ 67)

Top of the Tower

✉ Beekman, 3 Mitchell Place
☎ 212/355 7300

OLD MANHATTAN

The '21' Club (▶ 64)

The Jockey Club

✉ 112 Central Park South
☎ 212/757 9494

King Cole Bar

✉ St Regis Hotel, 2 E55th Street
☎ 212/753 4500

CAFFEINE

CAFFÈ REGGIO

The original, pre-coffee-bar craze, Roman rococo, bohemian espresso house.

✚ B10 ✉ 119 MacDougal Street ☎ 212/475 9557
🚇 A, B, C, D, E, F W4th Street

EUREKA JOE

This is no Starbucks (the Seattle chain), but a lovely, light lounge with couches and cake.

✚ C8 ✉ 168 Fifth Avenue
☎ 212/741 7500 🚇 L, N, R Union Square

JONATHAN MORR ESPRESSO BAR

Midtown's fanciest aluminium bean palace. Dig those cup sconces.

✚ E5 ✉ 1394 Sixth Avenue (57th Street) ☎ 212/757 6677
🚇 B, Q 57th Street

HOTEL BARS

OAK BAR

Classic city swank.

✚ E5 ✉ Plaza, Fifth Avenue (59th Street) ☎ 212/759 3000
🚇 N, R 5th Avenue

PEN TOP LOUNGE

Way up high, and glazed all round like a sputnik spacecraft on the roof. What views!

✚ E5 ✉ Peninsula, 700 Fifth Avenue (54th Street)
☎ 212/247 2200 🚇 N, R 5th Avenue

VODKA BAR

Teeny and *haute* style – feels like being trapped in a Bridget Riley canvas.

✚ D6 ✉ Royalton, 44 W44th Street ☎ 212/944 8844
🚇 B, D, F, 42nd Street

LITERARY BEER

PETE'S TAVERN

The 1864 Gramercy Park Victorian where O Henry wrote *The Gift of the Magi*.

✚ D9 ✉ 129 E18th Street
☎ 212/473 7676 🚇 N, R, 4, 6 Union Square

WHITE HORSE TAVERN

Here Dylan Thomas drank his last. A picturesque Village pub.

✚ B9 ✉ 567 Hudson Street
☎ 212/243 9260 🚇 1, 9 Christopher Street

BEER

D.B.A.

An East Village dive that takes beer more seriously than itself. What does it mean? – 'Doing Business As'.

✚ D10 ✉ 41 First Avenue
☎ 212/475 5097
🚇 F 2nd Avenue

HEARTLAND BREWERY

Loud, brash and central. Frat boys, pinstripes, office girls and brew.

✚ D9 ✉ 35 Union Square (16–17th Streets)
☎ 212/ 645–3400 🚇 Union Square

MCSORLEY'S OLD ALE HOUSE

Someone will show you this sawdust-floor tavern and tell you it's historic (1854).

✚ D10 ✉ 15 E7th Street
☎ 212/473 9148 🚇 6 Astor Place

PERFORMANCE

BROADWAY

The quintessence of glamour and sparkle, but the district was, until recently, lousy with porn palaces and clip joints. Now the Times Square redevelopment plan has removed the faint scent of danger and seedy neon charm, replacing it with Disney outposts and Condé Nast's new home. Between 42nd and 53rd Streets, and Sixth to Ninth Avenues.

OFF AND OFF-OFF

BAM

Or Brooklyn Academy of Music, which mounts major cutting-edge work in every discipline.
✚ Off map at I14　✉ 30 Lafayette Avenue, Brooklyn
☎ 718/636 4100　Ⓜ A, C Lafayette Avenue

THE FANTASTICKS

Not the name of the theatre, but of the popular musical that's been running since 1960.
✚ B9　✉ Sullivan, 181 Sullivan Street　☎ 212/674 3838　Ⓜ 1, 9 Christopher Street

JOSEPH PAPP PUBLIC THEATER

This has two stages and is named after its visionary and tireless founder.
✚ C10　✉ 425 Lafayette Street
☎ 212/598 7150　Ⓜ B, D, F Broadway/Lafayette Street

LA MAMA E.T.C.

The pace-setter downtown, having débuted many a triumph.
✚ D10　✉ 74A E4 Street
☎ 212/ 475 7710　Ⓜ F 2nd Avenue

MITZI E. NEWHOUSE & VIVIAN BEAUMONT

The Lincoln Center's two theatres stage established playwrights' work, often with famous actors.
✚ D4　✉ Lincoln Center
☎ 212/362 7600　Ⓜ 1, 9 66th Street

PERFORMANCE GARAGE

This is where the avant-garde Wooster Group mount their challenging multimedia performances.
✚ B10　✉ 33 Wooster Street
☎ 212/966 3651　Ⓜ C, E Spring Street

THE OPERA

AMATO OPERA

A hollowed-out East Village brownstone, mounting full-length grand opera in miniature.
✚ D10　✉ 319 Bowery
☎ 212/228 8200　Ⓜ F 2nd Avenue

THE METROPOLITAN OPERA

On a first night this is *so* glamorous. Never mind the singers – the Franco Zefirelli productions are the visual equivalent of Belgian cream truffles. Season: Oct–Apr.
✚ D4　✉ Lincoln Center
☎ 212/362 6000　Ⓜ 1, 9 66th Street

NEW YORK CITY OPERA

Occupies the auditorium next to the Met Sep–Nov and Mar–Apr. Offers newer works, operetta and the odd musical as well as the grands.
✚ D4　✉ Lincoln Center
☎ 212/870 5570　Ⓜ 1, 9 66th Street

Where to get information

New York Magazine The most colourful and gossipy of the lot, and easy to use.

New York Press The cheapest way to get information – pick up this determinedly downtown paper for free at shops, cinemas, etc.

New York Times May not contain deathless prose, but listings in its Friday Weekend section are good, and the Sunday reviews are readable.

New Yorker Far, far more than mere listings, of course. Its 'Goings on About Town' has sections on every cultural corner (even restaurants).

Time Out Now has a New York edition, indistinguishable in layout from its London mother with its very clear listings and comprehensive information.

Village Voice Its shrinking readership suggests it's lost its touch, though it's still famous – for the least user-friendly listings. And now it's free, too.

ON THE TOWN

Gay New York

The subject merits several books of its own. This is one of the best cities in which to be gay, with a thriving, pulsating community for both genders, and all in between. The city shares the honours with San Francisco for launching 'gay lib' in the US, with Stonewall (▶ 31) playing a major role, and it still leads the world in everything from AIDS activism to spawning gorgeous transvestites. Yes, if the Lady Bunny, Lipsynka and, of course, RuPaul mean anything to you, this city is going to feel very comfortable. All three girls are New Yorkers, and – if their busy schedules allow – all make large appearances at that annual celebration of vogueing and posing, Wigstock (▶ 60).

SHOWTIME

CAFÉ CARLYLE
The Upper East Side's absolutely elegant, pastel-coloured *boîte*.
➕ F4 ✉ Carlyle Hotel, Madison Avenue (76th Street) ☎ 212/744 1600 🚇 6 68th Street

THE DUPLEX
Cabaret minus attitude: less need to dress at this Village version of a torch singer's showcase.
➕ B9 ✉ 61 Christopher Street ☎ 212/255 5438 🚇 1, 9 Christopher Street

TATOU
There's carnival (Wednesday to Saturday) on Tatou's ornate crimson and gilt-framed stage, a dance floor and jazz all week – and a talented chef.
➕ F6 ✉ 151 E50th Street ☎ 212/753 1144 🚇 6 51st Street

COMEDY

BLUE MAN GROUP
After five years of this trio's exceedingly mucky (paint-, not porn-spattered) *Tubes*, everyone's still rolling in the aisles, kids included.
➕ C10 ✉ Astor Place Theatre, 434 Lafayette Street ☎ 212/254 4370 🚇 B, D, F Broadway Lafayette Street

CAROLINE'S COMEDY CLUB
More of the already-made-it than the up-and-coming play here, in theatreland.
➕ D5 ✉ 1626 Broadway (49th Street) ☎ 212/7574100 🚇 1, 9 50th Street

JAZZ

BLUE NOTE
You'll fork out a lot to catch a big name at this famed Village club. They all come to NYC, and most stop off here and/or at the Vanguard.
➕ C9 ✉ 131 W3rd Street ☎ 212/475 8592 🚇 A, B, C, D, E, F W4th Street

BRADLEY'S
Small, wood-panelled, cosy; there's a dinner-hour pianist, but it's best very late.
➕ C9 ✉ 70 University Place (11th Street) ☎ 212/228 6440 🚇 6 Astor Place

IRIDIUM
This upstart with cartoon décor is by Lincoln Center. Try Mingus Mondays.
➕ D4 ✉ 44 W63rd Street ☎ 212/582 2121 🚇 1, 9 66th Street

KNITTING FACTORY
Moderns play this relocated factory of cool; but also beboppers and funksters.
➕ B11 ✉ 74 Leonard Street (Broadway) ☎ 212/219 3055 🚇 1, 9 Franklin Street

VILLAGE VANGUARD
This basement is the *ne plus ultra* of the jazz dive, 60 years old in 1995, and thriving. If you take in only one gig, make it here.
➕ B9 ✉ 178 Seventh Avenue South (11th Street) ☎ 212/255 4037 🚇 1, 9 Christopher Street

CLUBBING

NELL'S
Nell Campbell's two-level lounge/naughty dancing club endures, attracting all ages and types.
✚ B8 ✉ 246 W14th Street ☎ 212/675 1567 Ⓜ A, C, E 14th Street

REBAR
A long, narrow, friendly Chelsea club, with a penchant for Britishness, and much enthusiasm on the dance floor.
✚ B8 ✉ 127 W16th Street ☎ 212/627 1680 Ⓜ A, C, E 14th Street

S.O.B.'S
Number one for the Latin beat is the tropically decorated 'Sounds Of Brazil' – also for African sounds, reggae and other island music.
✚ B10 ✉ 204 Varick Street ☎ 212/243 4940 Ⓜ 1, 9 Canal Street

WEBSTER HALL
The very big East Village place that used to be the coolest.
✚ D9 ✉ 125 E11th Street ☎ 212/353 1600 Ⓜ 6 Astor Place

MUSIC FOR YOUTH

BROWNIE'S
Nose to tail in Alphabet City, slackers catch the local heroes. If the band *du jour* isn't here, try No Tell Motel, next door.
✚ D10 ✉ 160 Avenue A (11th Street) ☎ 212/420 8392 Ⓜ F 2nd Avenue

CBGB & OMFUG
Long after giving birth to Yank punk rock, this teenage steam room has spread all over the block, with a sweet 'unplugged' café next door. (It stands for 'Country, Blue Grass, Blues, & Other Music For Uplifting Gourmandizers'.)
✚ C10 ✉ 315 Bowery ☎ 212/982 4052 Ⓜ F 2nd Avenue

CONEY ISLAND HIGH
On the youth block of St Mark's Place, this is the kids' favorite dive.
✚ D10 ✉ 15 St Mark's Place (First/Second Avenues) ☎ 212/674–7959 Ⓜ 6 Astor Place

MERCURY LOUNGE
A laid-back atmosphere attracts the most listened-to performers at their zenith of hotness.
✚ D11 ✉ 217 E Houston Street ☎ 212/260 4700 Ⓜ F 2nd Avenue

MUSIC FOR ALL

IRVING PLAZA
Medium-big people, ranging from They Might Be Giants to Paul Simon, play in this galleried Gramercy hall.
✚ D9 ✉ 17 Irving Place ☎ 212/777 6800 Ⓜ N, R, 4, 6 Union Square

MADISON SQUARE GARDEN
Hosts the rock giants (▶ 17).

TRAMPS
Great atmosphere for rootsy bluesy bands (the Meters are regulars) and indie rock.
✚ C8 ✉ 45 W21st Street ☎ 212/727 7788 Ⓜ F 23rd Street

Lesbian and Gay Pride Week

The week in late June around the anniversary of Stonewall – New York's first gay rights uprising – is Lesbian and Gay Pride Week, which no longer resembles a 1970s-style angry activists' march, but is an excuse for highly visible partying. The terrible toll of AIDS has not dented the spirits of the community it hit the hardest, but rather has reconfirmed it. For proof, attend another of the city's favourite events: the annual, celebrity-studded AIDS Danceathon.

To help differentiate between the thousands of gay clubs, bars, restaurants and so on, drop in for a chat at the Lesbian and Gay Community Center (✉ 208 W13th Street ☎ 212/620 7310), or call the Switchboard (☎ 212/777 1800).

FREE SUMMER ENTERTAINMENT

August in Manhattan

August is a wicked month in Manhattan, with temperatures regularly making triple figures (Fahrenheit), and — even worse — humidity that frizzes hair and soaks T-shirts as soon as you step outside. The street noise-level rises too, and so do tempers. It's no wonder New Yorkers desert the city every weekend. An entire culture revolves around summer rentals and summer shares, and whether you're a houseguest in the right place and whether your houseguests are the right houseguests, but this will probably pass most visitors by entirely. And so it should, because what really matters is how, every weekend for a whole month, the city belongs to you. Theatres and movie theatres are half empty; Central Park lacks its usual rollerblade traffic jams; it takes less than an hour to cross town in a cab and, best of all, you can get a table almost anywhere without reservations.

MUSIC

CENTRAL PARK SUMMER STAGE

A great free festival of such variety that everyone will want to see at least three events. Sponsors' concession stands ring the stage, and many people bring picnics.
🚇 F4 ✉ Naumberg Bandshell (72nd Street) ☎ 212/360 2777 🕐 Jun–Aug 🚇 C 72nd Street

LINCOLN CENTER OUT-OF-DOORS

By no means just music, this is an admirable summerlong fiesta of 100 or so varied events.
🚇 D4 ✉ 62nd/66th streets ☎ 212/872 5400 🚇 1, 9 66th Street

METROPOLITAN OPERA IN THE PARKS

They not only come out on 4 July, they also do a whole season of free park concerts
☎ 212/362 6000

THE NEW YORK PHILHARMONIC

As above.
☎ 212/721 6500 🕐 Jul–Aug

WORLD FINANCIAL CENTER

The Plaza has lots of free concerts, all season.

THEATRE

SHAKESPEARE IN THE PARK

This much-loved festival is mounted by the Public Theater and consists of two works per season. Though tickets are gratis, you must queue in the morning and can take only two.

🚇 F2 ✉ Delacorte Theater, Central Park ☎ 212/539 8750 🕐 Jul–Aug 🚇 B, C 81st Street

DANCING

MIDSUMMER NIGHT SWING

'Dances under the Stars' is the subtitle for this weekly public party.
🚇 D4 ✉ Lincoln Center Plaza ☎ 212/875 5400 🕐 Jun–Jul 🚇 1, 9 66th Street

FESTIVALS

THE FOURTH OF JULY

Celebrations kick off at the Stars and Stripes Regatta (✉ South Street Seaport ☎ 212/669 9400 🕐 3–4 Jul), with accompanying concerts on the pier. At night the New York Philharmonic plays in Central Park, with a firework finale (☎ 212/875 5030), and Macy's shoots millions of dollars into the sky over the Lower Hudson in a full half-hour of pyrotechnics (☎ 212/494 5432). Good vantage points get very crammed. Consider Brooklyn.

MUSEUM MILE FESTIVAL

Crowds perambulate Fifth Avenue, visiting museums for free.
🚇 G1–3 ✉ Fifth Avenue (82–102nd Streets) 🕐 6–9PM, Jun 🚇 4, 5, 6 86th Street

NINTH AVENUE INTERNATIONAL FOOD FESTIVAL

Culinary nirvana.
🚇 D4/D5/C6 ✉ Ninth Avenue (37/57th Streets) ☎ 212/581 7217 🕐 10AM–7PM, 3rd weekend May 🚇 C, E 50th Street

THIS SPORTING TOWN

WATCHING

THE GIANTS AND THE JETS

The former have more fans than the latter, though both these football teams play in the same stadium. However, most tickets are sold as season tickets.
✉ Giants Stadium, East Rutherford, NJ ☎ Giants: 201/935 8222. Jets: 516/538 6600 ⏰ Sep–Dec

THE ISLANDERS & THE NEW JERSEY DEVILS

These hockey teams have some NY following.
✉ Nassau Coliseum, Long Island ☎ 516/888 9000 ✉ Meadowlands ☎ 201/935 3900

KNICKERBOCKERS

Basketball may now have more New York fans than baseball, football and hockey, thanks to this heart-breaking team, who keep getting close – but no cigar. If you can get tickets you'll certainly see celebs – Spike Lee and Woody Allen are diehard fans.
✚ C7 ✉ Madison Square Garden ☎ 212/465 6741 ⏰ Oct–Apr 🚇 1, 2, 3 34th Street

NEW YORK RANGERS

This hockey team is worshipped both for winning the 1994 Stanley Cup, and for Mark Messier.
✚ C7 ✉ Madison Square Garden ☎ 212/465 6741 ⏰ Oct–Apr 🚇 1, 2, 3 34th Street

THE YANKEES AND THE METS

They play in different leagues and are very different propositions, the more so the more you know about baseball. In any case, a game at either can be a fun day.
✉ Shea Stadium, Flushing, Queens ☎ 718/507 8499; Yankee Stadium, ► 47 ⏰ Apr–Oct

DOING
See also page 59.

CYCLING

Join the Central Park pack. Rent clunky bikes from Loeb Boathouse (✉ Central Park near E74th Street ☎ 212/861 4137) and good machines from Metro Bikes (✉ 1311 Lexington Avenue at 88th Street ☎ 212/427 4450).

IN-LINE SKATING

Learn to brake at the Wollman Rink (✉ Fifth Avenue at 59th Street ☎ 212/517–4800). Then rent—or buy—from Peck & Goodie (✉ 919 Eighth Avenue at 54th Street ☎ 212/246–6123).

ROCK CLIMBING

If you already can, then bring your shoes for Central Park bouldering – or the wall at Manhattan Plaza Health Club if you're desperate (✉ 450 W43rd Street ☎ 212/594 0554). If you want to learn, the NYC Outward Bound Center runs classes (☎ 212/348 4867).

RUNNING

By far the most-run place in the city is the 1.58 mile Central Park Reservoir track. The New York Road Runners Club has an all-season schedule and welcomes visitors (☎ 212/860 4455).

Party runners

A festive New York tradition, most suited to a city where the gym is frequently the second home, is the New Year's Eve Central Park Runner's World Midnight Run. Beginning with a costume ball, culminating in fireworks, and with a five-mile race in the middle, this none-too-serious athletic event attracts thousands of weekend (or year-end) warriors, many dressed to party. The start line is Tavern on the Green, and advance registration is around $5 (☎ 212/860 4455), which includes admission to the ball. Not all entrants get around to running, say the organisers.

LUXURY HOTELS

Prices

The hotels on the following pages are in three categories. For a double room, expect to pay:
Luxury hotels – over $240
Mid-range hotels – $120–$240
Budget accommodation – under $120

Will it, won't it, will it, won't it...

Will the Mercer Hotel have opened yet? In 1996, the upstart SoHo Grand beat it to the finish to become the first hotel in SoHo, and practically the first note to open downtown. Most of the work on the Mercer Hotel, opposite the Guggenheim, was already complete when it ran into engineering and legal problems and had to stall its already much-publicized opening. Meanwhile, plans were proceeding apace for a new building to go in an empty lot on West Broadway near Grand Street. The Grand grew fast, and it's hard to imagine SoHo without it now. As for the Mercer... watch that space.

CARLYLE

Visiting minor European royalty holes up in this 38-storey patrician palace on the Upper East Side, and trust funders keep an apartment for when they're not wintering in Gstaad. It's *fin de siècle* perfection to behold.

F4 35 E76th Street
212/744 1600 Carlyle Restaurant, the Gallery, Café Carlyle, Bemelmans Bar 6 68th Street

FOUR SEASONS

This newest New York grand has two things in common with its namesake restaurant: absolute glamour and a household-name architect (I M Pei of the Paris Louvre pyramid). It's spacious to the point of inducing agoraphobia.

E5 57 E57th Street
212/758 5700 5757
B, Q 57th Street

THE MARK

This exquisite and peaceful townhouse-mansion, a couple of blocks from the park on the Upper East Side, features antiques and calm, goose-down pillows, palms, Piranesi prints, and (mostly) your own kitchen.

F3 25 E77th Street
212/744 4300 Mark's
6 77th Street

PLAZA

Oh, what can you say about this star of screen (*Plaza Suite*, etc), and page (Eloise, who lived here) and gossip column (Trump, who bought it and married Marla in it). The rooms aren't the best in town, but its profile is, and so is the location (corner of Fifth, across from the park).

E5 768 Fifth Avenue
212/759 3000 Palm Court, Oak Room, Edwardian Room, Gauguin N, R 5th Avenue

PLAZA ATHENÉE

Parisian splendour on the Upper East Side, this manageably sized (160-room) Forte French copy is known for its amazing duplex penthouses, its security (Diana, Princess of Wales has stayed here) and *comme il faut* service.

F4 37 E64th Street
212/734 9100
Le Régence N, R 5th Avenue

RITZ-CARLTON

Back on track after many renovations, the English-style (meaning wood panelling) R-C, at the other end of Central Park South from Essex House, shares those park views, for which you pay more. The elegantissimo Italian restaurant panders to wealthier guests.

E5 112 Central Park South 212/757 1900
Fantino B, Q 57th Street

ST REGIS

Home to the opulent Lespinasse restaurant (▶ 62) and the famous King Cole bar with its Maxfield Parrish mural, the St Regis is the very definition of calm elegance. Find Louis XV-style, marble bathrooms, fitness centre, and spiffy service.

E5 2 E55th Street (Fifth/Madison Avenues)
212/753–4500 6 51st Street

MID-RANGE HOTELS

FITZPATRICK

The sole US representative of the family-owned Dublin chain, this place on the easterly side of Midtown has the charm of the Irish in abundance. It stands out for service, good taste – and the perfect brunch.

✚ F5 ✉ 687 Lexington Avenue ☎ 212/355 0100 🍴 Fitzers Ⓜ 4, 6 59th Street

FRANKLIN

The first of Bernard Goldberg's remarkable, small but growing, collection of elegant boutique hotels that look like luxury but at a chain store price. Any sacrifice is in room size, not high-style details like cedar-lined wardrobes…

✚ G3 ✉ 164 E87th Street ☎ 212/369 1000 Ⓜ 4, 5, 6 86th Street

GRAMERCY PARK

Popular with the fashion set, BBC people and other Britons, this charmer offers the keys to the private, eponymous park, small, quiet, shabby rooms, and a great Cole Porter-esque piano bar. Has its own art festival.

✚ D8 ✉ 2 Lexington Avenue ☎ 212/475 4320 🍴 Restaurant Ⓜ 6 23rd Street

HOTEL BEACON

This Lincoln Center/ Central Park neighbour looks and feels far more expensive than it is. It has very spacious rooms with kitchenettes, cable TV, big wardrobes, and your own voice mail.

✚ E2 ✉ 2130 Broadway (75th Street) ☎ 212/787 1100 Ⓜ 1, 2, 3 72nd Street

MAYFLOWER

Hard to find fault with this classic. The décor's fresh, the location – by Lincoln Center/Columbus Circle – is perfect for pleasure, business and running (get a park view room and you'll never leave); service is nurturing. It's lovable.

✚ E4 ✉ Central Park West at 61st Street ☎ 212/265 0060 🍴 The Conservatory Ⓜ A, C, D 1 59th Street

MORGAN

Ian Schrager and the late Steve Rubell created the 1980s in the ultimate disco, Studio 54; they also created this, the first of three design-conscious hotels (the Royalton is number two; see also the Paramount, ➤ 86). The Andrée Putnam-designed monochrome suites have Mapplethorpe prints and are among the most private in NYC – there's no sign.

✚ D7 ✉ 237 Madison Avenue ☎ 212/686 0300 Ⓜ 6 33rd Street

SHOREHAM

The Franklin's younger midtown sister is a beauty. Grey, black and metallic décor, with cedar closets, CD players and VCRs in every room.

✚ E5 ✉ 33 W55th Street ☎ 212/247 6700 Ⓜ E, F 5th Avenue

WASHINGTON SQUARE

The Village's only hotel recently injected a lot of cash, so is very comfortable, despite the lack of bellboys and such..

✚ C9 ✉ 103 Waverley Place ☎ 212/777 9515 🍴 CIII Ⓜ 1, 9 Christopher Street

The Algonquin

The Algonquin is for ever associated with the only group of literary wits to be named after a piece of furniture: the Algonquin Round Table. Not quite the Bloomsbury Group, the *bon viveurs* achieved almost as much at the bar here as they did in the pages of the embryo *New Yorker*, with Robert Benchley, Dorothy Parker and Alexander Woollcott particularly well ensconced. The hotel's Rose Room still contains the very table, and the *New Yorker's* offices still decant straight into the hotel.

BUDGET ACCOMMODATION

B&Bs

Those who prefer real neighbourhoods, authentic experiences and behaving like a local may opt for a B&B. Often these are found in Brooklyn brownstones, where the host has an extra room. Others are empty apartments. The only imperative is to book ahead. Try:

Abode Bed and Breakfasts Ltd ✉

Box 20022, NY10028

☎ 212/472 2000

Bed and Breakfast Network of New York

✉ 134 W32nd Street, Suite 602, NY10001

☎ 212/645 8134

Inn New York

✉ 266 W71st Street, NY10023

☎ 212/580 1900

New World Bed and Breakfast

✉ 150 Fifth Avenue, Suite 711, NY10011

☎ 212/675 5600

Urban Ventures

✉ Box 426, NY10024

☎ 212/594 5650

CARLTON ARMS

The wackiest hotel in New York has lurid murals done by artist guests covering every surface. The comfort level's basic, but it's friendly. As it says on the business card: 'This ain't no Holiday Inn'.

✚ D8 ✉ 160 E25th Street ☎ 212/684 8337 🚇 6 23rd Street

EXCELSIOR

Overlooking the Natural History Museum, this is reminiscent of a faded boulevard hotel in Paris, perhaps in the 1950s. All the big, clean, fluorescent-lit rooms have kitchenettes and a great deal of blue in the décor.

✚ E2 ✉ 45 W81st Street ☎ 212/362 9200 🍴 Coffee shop 🚇 B, C 81st Street

GERSHWIN

'We're just at the edge of hip,' says the manager of this first New York Interclub hotel – Urs Jakob's decidedly arts-orientated string of superhostels. Art elevates the style of basic rooms, and bars, roof gardens and lounges encourage sociability.

✚ D8 ✉ 7 E27th Street ☎ 212/545 8000 🍴 Café 🚇 N, R 23rd Street

MILBURN

Such a friendly place you become immune to the mismatched furniture in the bargain suites. These have shabby corners, but tons of space and facilities, including kitchens.

✚ E2 ✉ 242 W76th Street ☎ 212/362 5476 🚇 1, 2, 3 72nd Street

OFF SOHO SUITES

It's ten blocks to SoHo (ditto the East Village) from here, which makes the location officially bad. This translates into spacious suites with marble bathroom, full kitchen, phone, TV, a/c, in an area which young and arty people often prefer. Décor is plasticky.

✚ C11 ✉ 11 Rivington Street ☎ 212/979 9808 🍴 Le Gourmet Deli, SoHo Suites Café 🚇 F 2nd Avenue

PARAMOUNT

The best deal in the city for the visually sensitive, this bears the stunning stamp of Philippe Starck, even in the famously tiny rooms. All fashionable budget-watchers stay here.

✚ D5 ✉ 235 W46 Street ☎ 212/764 5500 🍴 Restaurant; Dean & Deluca 🚇 C, E 50th Street

PARK SAVOY

The diametric opposite to the Paramount, the tiny rooms here are hideous to look at, a designer's never been near the place and there's a (very helpful) front desk staff of one. However, it's one block back from Central Park South, with rock-bottom rates.

✚ E5 ✉ 158 W58th Street ☎ 212/245 5755 🚇 B, Q 57th Street

SEAPORT INN

This fairly new conversion a block or two from the water has unobjectionable chain-hotel décor (it's a Best Western). The charm lies wholly in its situation.

✚ B12 ✉ 33 Peck Slip ☎ 212/766 6600 🚇 2, 3, 4 Fulton Street

NEW YORK
travel facts

ARRIVING & DEPARTING

Before you go

- All visitors to the United States must have a valid full passport and a return ticket. For countries participating in the Visa Waiver Program, a visa is not required, though you must fill out the green visa-waiver form issued on the plane. You are also required to fill out a customs form and an immigration form.

When to go

- The New York winter can be severe, with heavy snow, biting winds and sub-freezing temperatures from December to February. It can be an ordeal to get around.
- Spring is unpredictable – even in April, snow showers can alternate with 'shirtsleeves' temperatures' – but the worst of winter is over by mid-March.
- Outdoor events start in earnest in May.
- July and August are extremely hot and humid (with occasional heavy rain), driving many New Yorkers out of town. However, during this time queues are shorter, restaurant reservations optional, outdoor festivals at their peak, and the city seems rather exotic. Air-conditioning is universal, which helps.
- Autumn (fall) is generally thought the best time to visit. Warm temperatures persist into October (even November), with humidity dropping off in September.

Climate

- Average temperatures:
  Dec–Feb -2–6°C (29–43°F)
  Mar 1–8°C (34–47°F)
  Apr 7–16°C (45–61°F)
  May 12–21°C (54–70°F)

  Jun 17–27°C (63–81°F)
  Jul–Aug 20–32°C (68–90°F)
  Sep 16–24°C (61–76°F)
  Oct 11–19°C (52–67°F)
  Nov 6–13°C (43–56°F).

Arriving by air

- Most international flights arrive at JFK Airport in Queens, about 15 miles east of Manhattan. Fewer arrive at Newark, New Jersey, 16 miles west. Domestic flights arrive at La Guardia, Queens, 8 miles east.

JFK

- Taxi: $30, plus tolls and tip. Take only a licensed cab from the official ranks.
- Bus: Carey Airport Express Coach (☎ 718/632 0500), to six stops in Manhattan about every 30 minutes; Gray Line Air Shuttle (☎ 212/757 6840) shared minibus to any location.
- Helicopter: National Helicopter (☎ 800/645 3494), ten-minute trip to 34th Street East Heliport.

Newark

- Taxi: $30–45, plus tolls and tip.
- Bus: Carey Airport Express, see above; NJ Transit Airport Express 300 (☎ 201/762 5100), to the Port Authority every 15 minutes; Olympia Trails Airport Express (☎ 212/964 6233) to Penn Station, Grand Central and WTC every 20 minutes; Gray Line, as above.

Arriving by sea

- The *QE2* still sails into the Passenger Ship Terminal (✉ Twelfth Avenue at 50th–52nd Streets).

Arriving by train

- Commuter trains (Metro-North) use Grand Central Terminal

(✉ 42nd Street at Park Avenue; ☎ 212/532 4900). Long-distance trains (AMTRAK) arrive at Pennsylvania Railroad Station (✉ 31st Street at Eighth Avenue; ☎ 212/582 6875). PATH trains from the suburbs stop at several stations in Manhattan.

Arriving by bus
- Long-distance (Greyhound) and commuter buses arrive at the Port Authority Terminal (✉ 42nd Street Eighth Avenue; ☎ 212/564 8484).

Customs regulations
- Non-US citizens may import duty free: 1 quart (32fl oz.) alcohol, 200 cigarettes or 50 cigars, and up to $100-worth of gifts.
- Among restricted items for import are meat, fruit, plants, seeds and lottery tickets.

ESSENTIAL FACTS

Travel insurance
- It is essential to have adequate insurance coverage when travelling in the US, mainly because of the astronomical cost of medical procedures.
- A minimum of $1 million medical coverage is recommended.
- Choose a policy which also includes trip cancellation, baggage and document loss.

Opening hours
- Banks: Mon–Fri 9–3 or 3:30; some open longer, and on Saturday.
- Shops: Mon–Sat 10–6; many are open far later, and on Sunday; those in the Village and SoHo open and close later.
- Museums: hours vary, but Mon is the most common closing day.
- Post offices: Mon–Fri 10–5 or 6.

- Of course, in the city that never sleeps, you'll find much open round the clock.

National holidays
- 1 January; third Monday in January (Martin Luther King Day); third Monday in February (Presidents' Day); Good Friday (half day); Easter Monday; last Monday in May (Memorial Day); 4 July (Independence Day); first Monday in September (Labor Day); second Monday in October (Columbus Day); 11 November (Veterans' Day); fourth Thursday in November (Thanksgiving Day); 25 December.

Money matters
- The unit of currency is the dollar (= 100 cents). Notes (bills) come in denominations of $1, $5, $10, $20, $50 and $100; coins are 25¢ (a quarter), 10¢ (a dime), 5¢ (a nickel) and 1¢ (a penny, increasingly optional).
- Nearly all banks have Automatic Teller Machines (ATMs), which accept cards registered in other countries that are linked to the Cirrus or Plus networks. Before leaving home, check which network your cards are linked to, and ensure your personal identification number is valid in the US, where six-figure numbers are the norm.
- Credit cards are also a widely accepted and secure alternative to cash.
- US-dollar traveller's cheques function like cash in all but small shops; $20 and $50 denominations are the most useful. Don't bother trying to exchange these (or foreign currency) at the bank – it is more trouble than it's worth, and commissions are high.

Etiquette

- Tipping: waiters get 15–20 per cent (roughly double the 8.25 per cent sales tax at the bottom of the bill); so do taxi-drivers. Bartenders get about the same (though less than $1 is mean), and will probably 'buy' you a drink if you're there a while. Bellboys ($1 per bag), room service waiters (10 per cent), and hairdressers (15–20 per cent) should also be tipped.

- Panhandlers: you will need to evolve a strategy for distributing change to the panhandlers among New York's immense homeless population. Some New Yorkers give once a day; some carry pockets of pennies; some give food; others give nothing on the street, but contribute a sum to a homelessness charity.

- Smoking is no longer a matter of politeness: there are ever more stringent smoking laws in New York. Smoking is banned on all public transport, in taxis, offices, shops and in restaurants seating more than 35. (Many restaurants are relaxed about this law, however.)

Safety

- As in any big city, maintain an awareness of your surroundings and of other people, and try to look as if you know your way around.

- Do not get involved with street crazies, however entertaining they may seem.

- The subway is probably best avoided at night, and also the Lower East Side, Alphabet City east of Avenue C, the far west of Midtown and of Greenwich Village, and north of about 90th Street.

- Central Park is a no-go area after dark (except for performances),

and the Financial District is eerily deserted – it's generally best to avoid deserted places after dark.

- Apart from this, common-sense rules apply: conceal your wallet; keep the zip or clasp of your bag on the inside; and do not flash large amounts of cash, gold and diamonds, etc.

Women travellers

- New York women are street-wise and outspoken, so if someone's harrassing you, tell him to get lost – he'll be expecting it.

- Though less sleazy than in the past, the Times Square area is still miserable for women walking alone.

Places of worship

- Baptist: Memorial Baptist Church (✉ 141 W115th Street ☎ 212/663 8830). Tourists are welcomed (for a moderate charge) Sundays 10.45AM.

- Episcopal: Cathedral of St John the Divine (✉ 112th Street at Amsterdam Avenue; ☎ 212/316 7400 ◉ Services at 8, 9, 11AM, 7PM); Grace Church (✉ 802 Broadway/10th Street ☎ 212/254 2000 ◉ Services at 9 and 11AM).

- Jewish: Temple Emanu-El (✉ 1 E65th Street ☎ 212/744 1400 ◉ Services at 5:30PM).

- Methodist: Christ Church United Methodist (✉ Park Avenue at 60th Street ☎ 212/838 3036 ◉ Services 9 and 11AM).

- Roman Catholic: St Patrick's Cathedral (✉ Fifth Avenue at 50th Street ☎ 212/753 2261).

Students

- An International Student Identity Card (ISIC) is good for reduced admission to museums, theatres, tours and other attractions.

- Carry the ISIC or other photo ID at all times to prove you're over 21 if you're ' carded', or you could be denied admission to nightclubs or forbidden to buy alcohol.
- Under-25s will find it hard to hire a car.

Time differences

- New York is on Eastern Standard Time: -5 hours from the UK, -6 hours from the rest of Europe.

Toilets (restrooms)

- Don't use public restrooms on the street, in stations or subways.
- Public buildings provide locked bathrooms (ask the doorman, cashier or receptionist for the key), or use those in hotel lobbies, bars, department stores or restaurants.

Electricity

- American current is 110–120 volts AC, so many European appliances need transformers as well as adapters. Wall outlets (sockets) take two-prong flat-pin plugs.

PUBLIC TRANSPORT

Subway

- New York's subway system has 469 stations, many open 24 hours (those with a green globe outside are always staffed).
- Since the recent major clean-up, carriages are free of those famous dangerous-looking graffiti and are air-conditioned. Still, the system is confusing at first, and you will probably manage some mistakes.
- To use the subway, you need a $1.50 token (get a 'Ten Pak' to save time, if not money) or a multiple-journey Metrocard. Drop the token or swipe the card

to enter the turnstile; accompanying children under 44in tall ride free.
- Many stations have separate entrances for up- and downtown service, so ensure you're going the right way.
- Check that you are not about to get on a restricted-stop Express train that's going to whisk you to Brooklyn or the Bronx. Instead, take a 'Local' (a 'Brooklyn Bound Local' is a downtown-bound train stopping at all stations).
- If you ride at night, stay in the 'Off Hour Waiting Area' until your train arrives, then use the carriage with the conductor, in the middle of the train.
- Transit information ☎ 718/330 1234 ◉ 6AM–9PM

Bus

- Buses are safe, clean – and excruciatingly slow. The fastest are Limited Stop buses.
- Bus stops are on or near corners, marked by a sign and a yellow painted curb.
- Any length of ride costs the same as the subway, and you can use a token, a Metrocard or the correct change, which you deposit on boarding, next to the driver. Ask the driver for a transfer which entitles you to a free onward or crosstown journey for an hour after boarding using the intersecting services listed on the back.
- A bus map showing many of the 200 routes travelled by the 3,700 blue and white buses is available from token-booth clerks in subway stations, and is an essential accessory.

Taxis

- A yellow cab is available when the central number (not the 'Off Duty' side lights) on the roof is lit.

- All taxis display the current rates on the door, have a meter inside, and can supply a printed receipt.
- Drivers are notorious for (a) knowing nothing about New York geography, (b) not speaking English and (c) having an improvisational driving style.
- Tip 15 per cent. Notes larger than $10 are unpopular for short journeys.

MEDIA & COMMUNICATIONS

Telephones

- Public payphones are everywhere, and they nearly always work.
- Drop a 25¢ coin after lifting the receiver and before dialling to pay for a five-minute local call; an additional nickel or dime is requested at the end of that time.
- Most businesses have a toll-free 800 number, and practically all also have some version of touch-tone operated phone-answering computer, which is self-explanatory.
- To dial outside the 212 area, including 800 numbers, prefix the code with a '1'.
- Hotels may levy hefty surcharges, even on local calls, so use payphones instead.
- Prepaid phonecards were starting to become available at press time, and there are a few credit card phones.

Post offices

- The main post office (✉ Eighth Avenue at 33th Street ☎ 212/967 8585) is open 24 hours. Branches are listed in the Yellow Pages (◉ Mon–Fri 8–6, Sat 8–1).
- Stamps are also available from hotel concierges and vending machines in stores, for a 25 per

cent surcharge.
- Post letters in the blue metal mailboxes, or in the slots in office lobbies, air, train and bus terminals, or at post offices.

Newspapers

- The local papers are the broadsheet *New York Times* (with a huge Sunday edition) and the tabloids: the *Daily News* (also with a generously supplemented Sunday edition) and the *New York Post*. Also look for the respected *Wall Street Journal* and the pink-hued, gossip-heavy, weekly *New York Observer*.

Magazines

- As well as the *New Yorker*, *New York* and *Time Out* (➤ 79), you may also see the self-consciously hip *The Paper*, the glossy *Manhattan File* and the even glossier *Avenue*.

Radio

- New York's excellent National Public Radio station, WNYC, broadcasts classical and avant-garde music, jazz, news and cultural programming on FM 93.9 and AM 820.
- New York, like most US cities, is the home of the 'shock jocks' of talk radio. The most famous is Howard Stern, who broadcasts Mon–Fri 6–10AM on FM 92.3 WXRK.

Television

- Hotels usually receive the 75 channels available to cable subscribers at last count. 'Main stream' TV includes the national networks and cable stations, the Public Broadcasting Service and the premium cable channels, such as MTV, E! and CNN.
- In addition, there are bizarre

Manhattan access channels, culture from the City University of New York (CUNY), New York 1 (with its constant onscreen weather update) and plenty of home shopping, as well as the live drama of Court TV.

International newsagents

- Many newsstands sell foreign newspapers; Hotalings (✉ 142 W42nd Street; ☎ 212/840 1868) is particularly well stocked.

EMERGENCIES

Lost property

- Be realistic – you are unlikely to recover something you lose. But try the following: subway and bus ☎ 718/625 6200; taxi ☎ 212/840 4734; JFK ☎ 718/656 4120; Newark ☎ 201/961 2230.

Medical treatment

- If you are unfortunate enough to need medical attention, you will be extremely thankful you took out adequate insurance. Any medical practitioner will ask for your insurance papers and/or a credit card or cash payment, and medical care is very expensive.
- In the event of an emergency, the 911 operator will send an ambulance. If you have more time in hand, you may opt for a private hospital rather than the overtaxed city-owned ones.
- The Doctors on Call service (☎ 212/737 2333) is 24 hour.
- Dental Emergency Service (☎ 212/679 3966; 212/679 4172 after 8 PM).

Medicines

- Bring a prescription or doctor's certificate for any medications, in case of customs enquiries, as well as in the case of loss. Many drugs

sold over the counter in Europe are prescription-only in the US.

- Pharmacies open 24 hours include Duane Reade (✉ 485 Lexington Avenue, 47th Street ☎ 212/682 5338; or 224 W57th Street at Broadway ☎ 212/541 9708).

Emergency phone numbers

- Police, Fire Department, Ambulance ☎ 911.
- Crime Victims Hotline ☎ 212/577 7777.
- Sex Crimes Report Line ☎ 212/267 7273.
- Police, Fire Department, Ambulance for the deaf ☎ 800/342 4357.

Consulates

- Australia ✉ 636 Fifth Avenue, ☎ 212/245 4000.
- Canada ✉ 1251 Sixth Avenue, ☎ 212/586 2400.
- Denmark ✉ 825 Third Avenue, ☎ 212/223 4545.
- France ✉ 934 Fifth Avenue, ☎ 212/606 3600.
- Germany ✉ 460 Park Avenue, ☎ 212/308 8700.
- Ireland ✉ 515 Madison Avenue, ☎ 212/319 2555.
- Italy ✉ 690 Park Avenue, ☎ 212/737 9100.
- Netherlands ✉ 1 Rockefeller Plaza, ☎ 212/249 1429.
- Norway ✉ 825 Third Avenue, ☎ 212/421 7333.
- Sweden ✉ Dag Hammarskjøld Plaza, ☎ 212/751 5900.
- UK ✉ 845 Third Avenue, ☎ 212/752 8400.

TOURIST OFFICES

The New York Convention & Visitors' Bureau ✉ 2 Columbus Circle ☎ 212/397 8222 ◷ Mon–Fri 9–6; weekends 10–3.

INDEX

CityPack
New York

Written by   Kate Sekules
Edited, designed and produced by
     AA Publishing
Maps   © The Automobile Association 1996
Fold-out map © RV Reise- und Verkehrsverlag Munich · Stuttgart
     © Cartography: GeoData

Distributed in the United Kingdom by AA Publishing, Norfolk House, Priestley Road, Basingstoke, Hampshire, RG24 9NY.

ISBN 0 7495 1650 X

Published by AA Publishing (a trading name of Automobile Association Developments Limited, whose registered office is Norfolk House, Priestley Road, Basingstoke, Hampshire RG24 9NY. Registered number 1878835).

Colour separation by Daylight Colour Art Pte Ltd, Singapore
Printed and bound by Dai Nippon Printing Co (Hong Kong) Ltd.

Acknowledgements
The Automobile Association would like to thank the following photographers, picture libraries and associations for their help in the preparation of this book: Allsport UK Ltd 47a (D Strohueyer), 47b (O Greule); The Frick Collection 41b; The Mansell Collection Ltd 12; New York Convention & Visitors' Bureau, Inc 60; Rex Features Ltd 9; E Rooney 59.
The remaining pictures are held in the Association's own library (AA Photo Library) with contributions from: D Corrance 2, 6, 13a, 15, 16, 19, 21, 27b, 29a, 30, 33b, 35a, 40, 44a, 44b, 51, 52, 53; R G Elliott 1, 5b, 17, 20, 24a, 26, 27a, 28, 32, 34, 35b, 37a, 38a, 41a, 42, 43a, 43b, 45, 46, 49a, 55, 61b, 87a; P Kenward 5a, 7, 13b, 18, 23a, 23b, 24b, 25, 29b, 31a, 31b, 33a, 36, 37b, 38b, 39, 48, 49b, 50, 56, 57, 58, 61a, 87b.

Cover photographs
Main picture: Robert Harding Picture Library
Insets: Spectrum Colour Library; Zefa Pictures Ltd

COPY EDITOR *Karin Fancett*
VERIFIER *Joanna Whitaker*   INDEXER *Marie Lorimer*
SECOND EDITION UPDATED BY *OutHouse Publishing Services*

Titles in the CityPack series
- Amsterdam • Atlanta • Bangkok • Barcelona • Berlin • Boston •
- Brussels & Bruges • Chicago • Florence • Hong Kong • Istanbul • Lisbon •
- London • Los Angeles • Madrid • Miami • Montréal • Moscow • Munich •
- New York • Paris • Prague • Rome • San Francisco • Singapore • Sydney •
- Tokyo • Toronto • Venice • Vienna • Washington, D.C. •